Deadly Women
Volume 16

20 Shocking
True Murder Cases

Robert Keller

**Please Leave Your Review of This Book At
http://bit.ly/kellerbooks**

ISBN: 9798878731119

© 2024 by Robert Keller

robertkellerauthor.com

Table of Contents

Melanie Eam

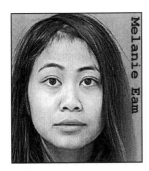

Melanie Eam and James Barry met in the middle of a heated battle, dodging bullets and running for cover, covering each other's backs as they engaged a formidable enemy. The pair were avid gamers and their love of role-playing games was what initially drew them together. Melanie was 18 then and having trouble with her high school grades. Fortunately for her, James was not only a gaming partner but a willing and conscientious coach. When it was time to turn off the X-Box and hit the books, he broached no excuses. It was largely due to his influence that Melanie gained her diploma. By then, she'd become a regular guest at the Loxahatchee, Florida home that James shared with his mother and stepfather. Often, she stayed the night.

Also living at the property at that time was a young man named Jeff Jarzabkowski, James's best friend since childhood. Like James and Melanie, Jeff was a keen gamer. The trio would spend hours together, hunched over their controllers, zapping insurgents and aliens and zombies. It was all great fun until it wasn't. Melanie, as it turned out, had a possessive streak. She was jealous of the friendship between James and Jeff. In fact, she demanded an end to it. She resented her boyfriend paying attention to anyone who wasn't her.

And so, the real-life battle lines were drawn with James caught in the middle. On the one hand, there was Melanie, hinting that she might break up with James if she had to play second fiddle. On the other, there was Jeff, warning his friend that Melanie had a dark side and that she wasn't to be trusted. James laughed off these warnings, of course. "Mel may be a bit overbearing," he chuckled, "But she's alright. I just wish the two of you would get along."

To Jeff, though, this was no laughing matter. Eighteen months into James's relationship with Melanie, he decided that he'd had enough. To him, his friend's girlfriend was perfectly personified by her gaming handle, "Hellraiser." Mel's avatar was also a fair representation of her character, in Jeff's estimation. It showed a succubus, a female demon, with its heart ripped out of its chest and held bleeding in its hand. In any case, Jeff wanted no part of Mel's histrionics. After making his apologies to James's mom and stepfather, he moved out of the Barry residence.

Round one in the battle for James's affection had gone to the possessive girlfriend. But if Mel thought that she had banished her rival, she was sorely mistaken. Jeff continued to visit when she wasn't around, something that always sent Mel into a tantrum when she found out. She issued an ultimatum, demanding that James make a choice between them. When he refused, she stormed off to bed.

It was now that James would discover that Jeff's warnings had not been overblown at all. While he slept that night, Mel slipped out of bed, crept down to the kitchen, and fetched a bottle of bleach. The contents of this container were poured into James's fish tank, condemning its dozens of occupants to an agonizing death. James woke the next morning to find his prized tropical fish floating dead on the surface. He immediately knew who was responsible and Mel made no attempt to deny culpability. "I did it to show you how much I love you," she said.

But this supposed show of devotion would backfire badly on Melanie Eam. James wasn't just furious at the loss of his pets, he was deeply concerned by Mel's behavior. Perhaps Jeff had been right after all. Maybe Mel really was unhinged. While his anger over his ruined aquarium was still up, he decided to end the relationship. Mel did not take the news well.

Melanie Eam had been James Barry's first serious girlfriend. Now, James was discovering the heartache that always accompanies the end of a love affair. Over the weeks that followed, he moped around the house, showing little interest in anything besides his nightly gaming sessions with Jeff. His friend assured him that he'd done the right thing but James wasn't so sure. He missed Mel terribly and longed to be with her. Gradually, his resolve began to waver. In early November 2017, he eventually gave in to his loneliness. He picked up the phone and asked Mel if he could see her. He was over the moon when she said yes.

James's reunion with Mel drew mixed reactions in his immediate circle. His mother and stepfather had always liked the girl, who'd never been anything but ultra-respectful towards them. Jeff was less pleased, although he kept his opinion to himself. It wasn't his place to tell James who he should be with. Perhaps he'd been too harsh on Mel. Maybe he should give her another chance.

But while Jeff might have been ready to let bygones be bygones, Mel was not in the mood for such indulgences. No sooner was she back in the picture when she started pressuring James again, insisting that he end his friendship with Jeff. James wasn't going to do that but he did come up with a compromise. Mel would have her time and Jeff would have his. James would do his best to keep the two of them apart.

This uneasy truce was never going to last. It would be put to its first (and ultimately, last) test on November 17, 2017. Jeff and James were in the midst of an online game that evening when, in the midst of the action, another player entered the fray...Hellraiser. This was a clear infraction of the rules the trio had agreed on. In disgust, Jeff threw down his game controller and stalked off to bed.

Just weeks after his reunion with Mel, James had been forced to face a harsh reality. He'd made a big mistake letting Mel back into his life. Mel hadn't changed. She was still the same obsessive, controlling individual who had driven him away in the first place. No matter how much hurt it might cause in the long run, he realized now that there was no future for them. With Mel still online, he clicked over into chat and started typing. "You'll always be special to me but this was a mistake. It's over Mel. I'm sorry. Maybe one day, when this is behind us, we can talk it through." Before Mel had a chance to respond and try to convince him otherwise, James logged out.

About an hour later, just after midnight, James was in bed and unable to fall asleep when there was a knock at the door. He went to answer it and was surprised to find Mel on his doorstep. "You said we could talk about it," she insisted, pushing past him and entering the house, where she stalked off toward the kitchen.

"Mel, it's late, can't we just..." James started to say before Mel cut him off.

"Do you love me?" she demanded.

"Mel, I..."

"Do you?" she insisted.

This was James's moment of truth. The next words out of his mouth would determine how this went. If he backed down now then the whole thing would start again, the possessiveness, the jealousy, the demands for attention. Faced with that prospect, James made a decision, one that would have catastrophic results.

"The truth, Mel, is that I don't love you. I did once but not anymore. This just isn't working. I hope that you can understand and that we can still be friends."

It was the typical "let me down easy" speech, with the exception that James meant what he was saying. Mel, though, wasn't listening. She was rummaging through a kitchen drawer. When she turned around she was holding a 13-inch carving knife. Without saying a word, she swung at him.

The first swing nicked James on the wrist, creating a graze that he hardly noticed. The second was deeper but still barely a nick. "Mel, stop," James begged, warding off the next lunge, "Let's talk about this." But Mel wasn't stopping. Blinded by rage, she continued swinging with the knife, inflicting six superficial wounds on her boyfriend's arms as he tried to defend himself. Then, suddenly, she shifted her grip on the knife handle and thrust the blade rather than arcing it.

The move caught James by surprise. Before he could even react, the knife had pierced his skin. Directed upward under the ribcage, it sliced through flesh, inflicting massive damage as it penetrated the left ventricle of the heart. James staggered back, mortally wounded, the heft of the knife still protruding from his chest. Mel, perhaps realizing what she'd done, turned and fled.

Jeff Jarzabkowski was sound asleep in bed when he was awakened by a crash and then the sound of someone crying out in pain. The sight that greeted him as he opened his eyes must have convinced Jeff that he was still asleep, afflicted by a nightmare. James had staggered into the room, clutching his chest and gasping for help. Impossibly, there appeared to be a knife sticking out from his chest. And the blood, so much of the stuff, welling out from between his friend's fingers.

Jeff was out of bed in a single movement. He caught James just before he collapsed to the floor. Jeff screamed for help. His cries were answered by Guy Hand, James's stepfather. Guy immediately started CPR but every breath that he exhaled into his stepson's lungs was gushing out through the ugly wound in James's chest. "Call 911!" Guy yelled to his wife. Unfortunately, it was already too late.

James Barry was already dead by the time paramedics arrived. That made this a murder and investigators soon had a suspect to focus on. The problem was that Melanie Eam was gone. She'd quit town, destination unknown. It would be three days before detectives tracked her to her family home in Silver Spring, Maryland. Taken into custody, Melanie made no pretense at innocence. She admitted stabbing James, saying that she'd done so in a fit of rage after he'd ended their relationship via a text message. "That set me off," she said. "He could, at least, have had the decency to do it in person."

By the time the matter came to trial, however, Melanie Eam's defense team had concocted a new version of events. They now claimed that it was Guy Hand who had stabbed James. According to this narrative, Melanie and Guy had gotten into an argument. James had stepped in to break it up and had been accidentally stabbed in the resulting melee. As unlikely as this scenario seemed, it struck a chord with the jurors. They were unable to reach a unanimous verdict. A mistrial was declared.

And so to the second trial, beginning in January 2019. This time around, the jury was not convinced by Melanie's tall tale of an altercation that resulted in an accidental stabbing. She was found guilty of second-degree murder and sentenced to 50 years in prison. Should she serve her full term, Melanie Eam will be in her seventies by the time she is released.

Lauren Stuart

Lauren Stuart was 42 years old and the mother of two adult children. She was also stunningly beautiful, a wife to Dan, and a devout Jehovah's Witness. Living in picturesque Keego Harbor, Michigan, Lauren presided over a beautiful and ordered home. She had a large circle of friends, most of them from her church, and was close to her family. Her husband had a good job as a software engineer at the University of Michigan Medical School. His crowning achievement was a revolutionary computer program that was able to detect early signs of heart disease. Those who knew Lauren considered her to be particularly blessed.

But here's the thing about gilded lives, quite often the gloss is only a thin sheen, hiding the hurt that lingers just below the surface. In Lauren's case, there was childhood trauma, in the form of sexual abuse by a relative. It had left her prone to depression and anxiety, conditions that had gone untreated due to her church's stance on such things. The power of prayer and of community were Lauren's only stanchions against the demons that plagued her. Still, she'd always found those things to be adequate.

Dan Stuart, although also a believer, was less devout than his wife. With an IQ in the range of 165, Dan was a recognized genius. He'd passed those good genes on to his children. Steven, 27, was a computer whizz like his dad. Bethany, at 24, was a graphic designer and a talented artist. Despite their obvious abilities, though, neither of the children had attended college. This, again, was down to the family's religious beliefs. The church elders frowned on higher education. To them, university campuses were dens of iniquity, where sex and drugs and alcohol were prevalent and where subversive ideas were imposed on impressionable young minds. Church members were actively discouraged from sending their children to college. To go against this ruling was to risk excommunication from the church.

Given these competing agendas, it was inevitable that there would be a showdown at some point. Dan and Lauren were still debating how to resolve the issue when there was a summons from the church hierarchy. Their presence was required at a meeting. Lauren had told one person too many about their plans to send their children to college. Word had reached the elders and now an explanation was required. The meeting would turn out to be a thinly disguised dressing down. The Stuarts were told in no uncertain terms that their plans were objectionable to the church. The consequences were also made clear. Proceed down this path and they would be cast out.

Lauren Stuart might well have buckled at this point and given in.
The church was her life and the idea of losing her place in it was
unthinkable. But Dan was not so easily bowed. His children were
gifted. He knew that. He was not going to sacrifice their futures
over church politics. As far as he could tell, the ruling had no basis
in scripture. Where was it written that one should subjugate one's
God-given talents? Surely the opposite was true? And so, Dan
informed the church elders of his decision. His children would be
attending college and they could do their damnedest. Their
damnedest, as it turned out, was to eject the entire family from the
faith, an act known in the Jehovah's Witness church as
"disfellowshipping."

The Stuarts were not exactly surprised by the actions of their
church. They had, after all, been warned that this was the likely
outcome. However, they were surprised by the far-reaching
implications of their shunning. Church members they'd known for
years, people they considered friends, suddenly turned their backs
on them. Even Lauren's family cut them off. This was easier for
Dan to handle than for Lauren. He, at least, had his colleagues at
the university. She was stuck at home, with no friendships outside
the church. Cut off from those connections, lonely and alone, old
demons began to resurface.

Lauren's method of dealing with her unwanted isolation was
simple. She kept herself busy. All of her life, people had been
telling her that she ought to have been a model. Now, she revisited
that ambition. After answering an ad, she attended a photoshoot
that went so well that there was an immediate offer of paid work.
Lauren also applied herself to redecorating the family home,
carrying out all of the work herself, even painting the roof. Her

main passion, though, was Bible study. She may have been ejected from the church but that did not make her any less of a Christian. A good portion of each day was spent reading and researching the scriptures. Soon, she began to believe that she had found some hidden meaning in them.

The message that Lauren had uncovered was troubling. It spoke of the end of days, of the final battle between good and evil, of Armageddon. Lauren, of course, knew all about this calamitous event. It was an important pillar of her church's doctrine. It was widely taught that members of the faith would be guaranteed admittance to heaven that day, even as the unbelievers were cast into the pit of fire.

This teaching was deeply troubling to Lauren. Since she and her family had been cast out from the church, they would be numbered among the heathen. That meant that they were doomed, condemned to hell. Their only hope of redemption was if they were to die before the day of reckoning arrived. Lauren was not at all certain that would happen. Her interpretation of the scriptures suggested to her that the end was nigh.

These are not the thoughts of a rational person. But Lauren had been teetering on the edge of a mental breakdown for some time now and her disfellowshipping from the church had proved to be the final nudge that tipped her over the edge. On the outside, she maintained her normal routine, running an orderly house, exercising, doing the shopping, attending photoshoots. In secret, though, she was doing research. The searches she was entering into Google and YouTube would have worried anyone who knew about them. Lauren was learning how to use her husband's Glock firearm. She was also exploring the most efficient ways to end her life.

On the afternoon of February 15, 2018, Bethany Stuart was dozing in her bedroom when her mother entered. Lauren was carrying a gun, the same Glock that she'd spent the last few weeks learning about. She also had a clear mission in mind. She was going to save her daughter's soul. Without so much as pausing to think about what she was doing, she picked up a pillow from the bed and placed it over Bethany's face. Then she leveled the pistol and pulled off two shots, ending her daughter's life. She felt no remorse over what she'd done. A mother should be prepared to sacrifice for her children and Lauren had not wavered when called upon.

Lauren Stuart had planned this whole operation in great detail. She was unflustered as she left her daughter's room, calm as she walked down the stairs. Her son would be arriving soon. She'd invited him. Steven had no inkling that anything was amiss as he entered the house. Lauren asked him to help her with something in the spare bedroom. He'd just entered when she shot him in the back of the head.

Her children were dead, redeemed from the fires of hell. Now Lauren sat down to wait for her husband to arrive from work. Dan was shot to death in the basement before Lauren headed back upstairs. Her final act before killing herself was to shoot the family dog. Then she walked to the foot of the stairs, sat down on the second step, and placed the barrel of the Glock against her forehead. A single bullet put an end to her suffering. It was the exact method she'd read about online.

The bodies of the Stuart family were discovered the next day when police officers responded to a call by Lauren's cousin. Lauren had sent her a rather disconcerting text. "I became evil," she'd written. "I took my husband and kids so they don't have to feel my selfish act." Lauren had also left behind a suicide note. "I allowed evil into my heart when I chose not to accept God's free love and it made me sick inside," she wrote. "I killed my family because I know my death would stumble them. At least now they will not suffer and will be resurrected into love forever in peace."

Terrie Robinson

When police officers in Greenville, Mississippi responded to an emergency call on March 2, 2011, they had no idea what they were walking into. The caller had simply said that an infant had been hurt. She'd given an address at the Riverwalk Apartments. Officers arrived to find the occupant of that apartment, 24-year-old Terrie Robinson, sitting calmly in a chair, muttering to herself, her hands playing out a nervous dance in her lap. Meanwhile, the overwhelming stench of seared flesh pervaded the residence. Robinson was unresponsive to questions and so one of the cops carried out a search, heading first for the kitchen, where the smell was coming from. His eyes fell immediately on the electric oven. Something was inside. He could see it through the glass. The officer stepped forward and levered the door open. Then he took a step back in horror. Inside the oven was the badly seared corpse of a toddler.

Even to patrol officers used to dealing with the worst of human traits and behavior, this was a shocking crime. As one of the cops cuffed Terrie Robinson and read her rights to her, the other returned to the police cruiser to summon backup and a forensic unit. Soon the lot of the building would be jammed with police vehicles and crime scene tape was being strung. It was just after midnight when Washington County Coroner Methel Johnson arrived to begin the gruesome task of examining the seared remains.

The victim of this dreadful crime was Tristan Robinson, the three-year-old son of Terrie Robinson. An autopsy would later determine that the child had died of "thermal heat." He had literally been cooked alive. The child had also suffered a serious head fracture and that, at least, offered a modicum of solace. It is possible that he was unconscious when his mother placed him in the oven and turned up the heat. On the other hand, the medical examiner could not rule out the possibility that he might have struck his head while thrashing around inside his red-hot coffin, trying to escape. That idea is just too terrible to contemplate.

This was not a crime that required a great deal of detective work. The killer was in custody and did not deny responsibility. The more pertinent question was why. Why would a mother inflict such a terrible death on her child, her own flesh and blood?

The answer, unfortunately, is a common one in cases like this. It mirrors infamous instances of parricide like those committed by Andrea Yates and Dena Schlosser. Terrie Robinson was afflicted by an undiagnosed mental illness. And her condition was made worse by religious mania. In the weeks leading up to the murder, Terrie had complained of hearing voices and being possessed by demons. She professed that she was receiving communications from both God and Satan. Sadly, the people she turned to for help failed to provide her with the care she so clearly needed.

We know very little about Terrie Robinson's life other than that she was a native Mississippian born in October 1986, one of twins. She appears to have had a difficult childhood and an even more fraught adolescence. As an adult, she was promiscuous, running through a series of short-term relationships and numerous one-night stands. This inevitably resulted in her falling pregnant and delivering a daughter. The identity of that child's father was known to her. This was not the case when she gave birth to Tristan in 2007.

Although this barely qualifies as a talking point in our modern age, it appears to have been a big deal to Terrie. She wanted her child to know who his father was and contacted the man she believed was responsible. When this man denied paternity, she pestered him until he agreed to take a test. It came back negative.

This turned out to be a major source of distress for Terrie. Over the months and years of her son's life, she became increasingly agitated about it. Turning to the scriptures for answers, she somehow developed the idea that she had committed the ultimate, unforgivable sin. She was certain that she was bound for hell. When she raised this idea with friends and family, they assured her that she was being ridiculous, that she was a good mom and was raising two beautiful children in challenging circumstances. This appears to have been of little solace to Terrie.

And so Terrie turned for support to her church, issuing a plea for help that would ultimately go unanswered. She was met instead by the assertion that she was an adulteress, unworthy of God's grace. She was urged to pray for forgiveness anyway, which she did, frequently and fervently. Unfortunately, this only served to exacerbate the problem. Her supplications turned into two-way conversations with God. She became convinced that he was demanding a sacrifice of her, the purification of her son, by fire.

Eventually, those voices became so strident that Terrie could no longer ignore them. Yet even now, she appears to have been looking for a way out. On the night that she committed her terrible, desperate act, Terrie Robinson called several acquaintances and begged them to come over, to sit with her. No one responded to that call. They all assumed that she'd been drinking and told her to sleep it off. Instead, Terrie Robinson went into the kitchen and turned up the heat on the electric oven. Then she walked to the apartment's single bedroom and fetched her son from his crib...

Terrie Robinson made no effort at all to evade the consequences of her crime. After killing Tristan, she dialed 911 and waited calmly for the police to arrive. In the aftermath of the murder, her twin sister would assert that Terrie was an excellent mom, who loved her children, that people should not rush to judgment. Be that as it may, an innocent child had been killed in a quite horrific manner. There was a price to be paid. The prosecutor believed that the price should be death by lethal injection. Spooked by this, Terrie's public defender convinced her to take a plea.

In May 2012, Terrie Robinson entered a guilty plea to first-degree murder and accepted a term of life in prison without parole. This was a controversial sentence, one that failed to appease lobbyists on either side of the political divide. Commentators to the right argued that a crime this horrendous could only be attenuated by the death penalty.

To the left, the argument was that Terrie Robinson did not deserve jail time at all. This was a woman with serious mental issues. Clearly, she was schizophrenic. Her place was in an institution, with medication and psychiatric help. She should be free to rejoin society once a mental health professional deemed it safe for her to do so.

There are valid points on both sides of the debate and precedents (such as the Yates and Schlosser cases, mentioned above) where the courts have followed a different path to justice. But while we contemplate the fairness (or otherwise) of Terrie Robinson's sentence, let us not forget that a three-year-old child lost his life here. Tristan Robinson's last moments on this earth were beyond what anyone should ever have to endure.

Maria Barbella

The year was 1892 and in New York City the turnstiles of Ellis Island were clicking out an up-tempo rhythm as they admitted hopeful migrants from the Old World. Italy and Ireland were the most common points of origin that year, with as many as 247,000 settlers incoming from the former country. Among this throng, the arrival of Michele Barbella, his wife Filomena, and their 24-year-old daughter, Maria, went mostly unnoticed. The family settled into a tenement apartment in the Mulberry Bend slum, an area of Manhattan's Little Italy. Shortly after, Maria, who spoke no English, found a job as a seamstress at Louis Graner & Co., a clothing manufacturer.

Maria was a somewhat plain girl, painfully shy, and in serious danger of being left on the shelf in the marital stakes. She had never had much attention from men and was therefore surprised when one started paying her attention. His name was Domenico Cataldo and he ran a shoeshine booth at the corner of Canal and

Lafayette Streets. This just happened to be on Maria's route to work. Every day, Cataldo would call out a greeting as she passed and every day Maria would blush deeply, duck her head, and rush past. It was weeks before she finally plucked up the courage to respond. After that, she started leaving home a little earlier, giving her time to dawdle a few minutes and chat with her newfound friend.

Domenico Cataldo was not a handsome man. He was short and stubby and at 27, he already had a receding hairline. His face was also badly pockmarked and his nails were permanently blackened by boot polish. But Cataldo had at least one thing going for him with the ladies. He talked a good game and, to the naïve Maria, he seemed charming and sophisticated. He was also from the same region of Italy as her, so there was an instant connection. "I'm looking for the right girl to marry," he told Maria. "And the one that I choose will want for nothing. I already have over $900 saved."

Maria hoped fervently that Cataldo would choose her. She started stopping at his booth on her way home, allowing him to escort her the last few blocks. Excitedly, she told her parents about Domenico, mentioning that he was well-off and that he was from the Basilicata region of Italy. Michele and Filomena were keen to meet the man who had so impressed their daughter but Cataldo was elusive, always finding some excuse to avoid an introduction. Eventually, Michele Barbella began to suspect that he must be hiding something. After yet another dinner invitation was declined, Michele forbade Maria from ever seeing Cataldo again.

Maria was heartbroken by this outcome. But she was a dutiful daughter and so she accepted her father's ruling. She began walking a different route to work, avoiding Cataldo's shoeshine booth. This worked for a few weeks but then, one day in March 1895, Maria found Cataldo waiting for her outside the factory gates.

The sight of him made Maria's heart leap for joy. She almost replied when he called out his customary greeting but then she remembered her father's directive and brushed past without responding. It was the same on the second day and again on the day that followed and on the one after that. Finally, after ten days of this charade, Cataldo blocked Maria's path and insisted that she hear him out. The words, he spoke were music to her ears. "Maria," he said, "I can't live without you. Will you be my wife?"

Maria felt as though her feet were hardly touching the paving stones as she rushed home to tell her parents the good news. Domenico had proposed. Not only that but he had agreed to meet with them, to ask formally for her hand in marriage. That meeting was to take place a few days hence, on March 28.

On the day in question, Cataldo asked Maria to meet him at a tavern on Chrystie Street, about halfway between their respective residences. From there, they'd walk together to meet her parents. Maria, of course, agreed to the arrangement and gladly accepted the soda that Cataldo offered when she arrived at the bar. Thirsty from her walk, she drank deeply. A few moments later, she began to feel dizzy. Everything swam out of focus. The room appeared to be spinning.

Maria Barbella had just been drugged, slipped a Mickey, given a roofie in modern parlance. Now, her concerned fiancé escorted her from the bar and suggested that they walk to his room, where she could lie down to recover her senses. This, of course, was a ruse. Once there, he tore off Maria's clothes and had his way with her. In her drugged state, Maria was powerless to resist. In fact, she passed out during the ordeal. When she awoke, groggy and with a pounding headache, Cataldo sarcastically congratulated her on finally losing her virginity.

Overcome with shame, Maria staggered home and told her mother what had happened. Filomena was outraged and immediately set off to find Cataldo. Tracking him to his favorite bar, she gave him a dressing down in front of his friends. "You know the traditions of our people," she insisted. "You are obligated to marry Maria for the sake of her honor. Confronted by an incensed Italian mama, Cataldo wasn't stupid enough to argue. He sulkily agreed to make good on his promise.

Over the days that followed, however, the elusive Lothario was back to his old tricks. He continued to vacillate, refusing to be tied down to a wedding date. Finally, on April 20, he admitted to Maria that he would never marry her, claiming that he was already wed, with a wife and children back in Italy. Maria was crushed.

But Filomena wasn't giving up as easily, not when her daughter's honor was at stake. She was convinced that Cataldo was lying to avoid his obligation. On April 26, she and Maria tracked him down to Mancuso's Saloon on East 13th Street. There, Filomena would make one last plea to his better nature. She should have known by now that Cataldo had no such quality.

Surrounded by his drinking buddies, Cataldo was in particularly belligerent mood that day. He laughed in Filomena's face when she asked if he was a man of honor. Then he said that he would marry Maria if her parents paid him a $200 "dowry," an impossible sum for poor immigrants. Finally, in exasperation, Filomena stormed off, uttering some choice insults as she did. These seemed only to amuse Cataldo and his friends further.

Maria had not spoken a word during this entire encounter but now she stepped forward, inclined her head towards the man who had raped her and whispered something in his ear. Cataldo's companions couldn't hear what she said but they certainly heard Cataldo's response. "Marry you?" he chuckled. "Only a pig would marry you."

These were the last words that Domenico Cataldo spoke in this world. As Maria straightened up, the bystanders noticed a flash of silver in her hand. The straight razor was drawn across Cataldo's throat, cutting deep, opening up a gash from ear to ear. The spurt of blood was prodigious, spattering those standing nearby. Cataldo staggered to his feet, his hands flailing at his mutilated neck in a useless effort to stanch the flow of blood. By now, Maria was running for the door. Cataldo lurched out after her, leaving a thick ribbon of blood in his wake. He collapsed in the gutter of East 13th Street, convulsed for half a minute and then lay still.

Arrested and charged with murder, Maria Barbella was held at the
New York Prison, a.k.a. The Tombs, remaining there until her trial
in July 1895. She was represented by two novice attorneys, Amos
Evans and Henry Sedgwick, and adjudicated by an all-male jury.
The judge, John W. Goff, was openly antagonistic towards her,
explicitly instructing the jurors that they were not to go easy on
the accused just because she was a woman. With all of these
factors taken into account, it was hardly surprising when Maria
was found guilty as charged. Judge Goff sounded almost gleeful as
he passed sentence of death by electrocution.

After sentencing, Maria Barbella was transported to Sing Sing
prison to await her date with the executioner. As things stood, she
would be the first woman to be put to death by this method. But
the case had attracted widespread publicity and much support for
Maria among the general populace. Governor Levi P. Morton was
inundated with letters begging him to intervene. One particularly
prominent supporter of Maria Barbella was Cora Slocomb, an
American who had married an Italian count and was now titled
Countess Savorgnan. The noblewoman traveled back to the United
States to take up the fight for Maria. It was largely due to her
efforts that an appeal was granted.

Maria Barbella's second trial was considerably longer than the
first, with much of the testimony focused on the accused's state of
mind. Evidence was presented by the defense claiming that Maria
suffered from epilepsy and had committed the murder while in the
grip of an epileptic fugue. This state of affairs was brought about
by Cataldo's ill-treatment, her attorney claimed. The jury was

urged to find her not guilty and it duly obliged, acquitting her of all charges.

Reprieved from death row, Maria Barbella would eventually get her wish of a husband and family when she married an Italian immigrant named Francesco Bruno in November 1897, and had a son by him. Unfortunately, the marriage did not last. A 1902 census places Maria back in the cramped Mulberry Bend apartment, living with her parents. From that point on, there is no further record of her life.

Theresa Petto

The year was 2007 and Theresa Petto was attending her high school reunion in Kalamazoo, Michigan. The evening had been a chastening one for the recently divorced mother-of-two. All of her old school friends seemed to have moved on to better things, to careers and happy marriages. Theresa, meanwhile, was washed up at 35, afflicted by rheumatoid arthritis, living off disability checks and child support. The disparity left her feeling depressed and decidedly inadequate. She was ready to skulk off into the night when she ran into Brent Kik.

Brent had been a classmate of Theresa's back in the day. He and Theresa had been on friendly terms back then, although there was nothing more to it than that. They'd certainly never dated. Now, though, he was a sight for sore eyes, handsome and athletic, looking dapper in his expensive Italian suit. He told her that he was a VP for a printing company, making decent bank, living the good life, still single. That last snippet was of particular interest to

Theresa. When Brent asked if she wanted to join him for a
nightcap after the party, she almost tripped over her tongue saying
yes.

That was how it began. The pair started seeing each other with
Brent sometimes staying the night but never giving any hint that
he wanted to take the relationship further. Then, in 2010,
something happened that changed everything. Theresa was
pregnant. Thereafter, she started pressuring Brent to live up to his
responsibilities. Those calls became ever more strident after the
birth of the couple's daughter in June of 2011. Theresa wanted
them to move in together, to be a family. Brent wasn't keen on the
idea. He was happy to pay child support and to be involved in
raising his daughter. What he didn't want was a wife and kids.

This would end up becoming a major bone of contention between
the pair. There were frequent fights, often getting so heated that
Theresa threw Brent out, telling him never to return. But Brent
always came back. He wasn't sure how he felt about Theresa
anymore but he was determined to be there for his daughter.

And then, on June 4, 2015, there was a tragic turn of events. That
was the day that Theresa Petto called 911 and told the dispatcher
that her baby wasn't breathing and was turning blue in the face.
Paramedics rushed to the scene but were unable to resuscitate the
infant. She was declared dead at the scene. A postmortem
examination found that the child had suffered a skull fracture,
although Theresa vehemently denied causing the injury. The
baby's death was ultimately attributed to Sudden Infant Death
Syndrome.

In the aftermath of this tragedy, Theresa descended into a deep depression. She suffered severe mood swings, weepy one moment, manic and aggressive the next. She became increasingly dependent on Brent for emotional support. At a time when he was trying to come to terms with the death of his daughter, Theresa was clinging to him, pressuring him to make their relationship more permanent. In the end, she only succeeded in driving him away. Shortly after the death of their child, he told her that it was over.

Anyone who has ever been in love, has experienced the agony of a broken heart. It hurts like hell but eventually, you pick yourself up, dust yourself off, move on. Years later, you probably look back and chuckle at your foolishness. You may even realize that the break-up was the best thing that could have happened to you.

But Theresa Petto was not like most people. Theresa had a vindictive streak a mile wide. To friends, she ranted and raved about the man who had abandoned her in the depths of her despair, who had walked away when she needed him most. Those rants would reach a crescendo when she heard that Brent was dating someone else.

Brent's new love interest was a work colleague named Rachel Drafta. At 25, Rachel was 18 years younger than Theresa. She was also beautiful, well-educated, refined. None of this went down well with Theresa. Her rage had now shifted. No longer was it directed at Brent. It was focused entirely on his new love. She ranted constantly about the woman who had stolen her life, taken her man, who was living in her house, sleeping in her bed. This, even though she and Brent had never cohabitated.

To Theresa's friends, the solution to her problem was obvious. Brent had moved on. She needed to do the same. But Theresa wasn't backing down. If anything, she was upping her game. She began stalking her ex, driving past his house at all hours of the day and night. She started keeping a journal, obsessively tracking Brent and Rachel's movements. More worryingly, she began assembling what can only be described as an "abduction kit." This included duct tape, cable ties, rubber gloves, a machete, a revolver, and lots of ammo. Slowly, over the weeks that followed, she began crafting her journal entries into a list, a "to-do" list for a murder.

June 24, 2015, marked a sad anniversary. It was four years exactly from the day that Theresa Petto's daughter died. It was also the day that Theresa had decided to put her plan into action, the plan that she believed would win back her former lover. Early that morning, Theresa got into her car and drove to the Portage, Michigan neighborhood where her nemesis, Rachel Drafta, lived with her parents. Parking her vehicle a couple of blocks away, she proceeded on foot to Rachel's street. There, she waited in the shadows until Rachel emerged from her house, just after 7:20.

Theresa had played out this scenario many times in her head. In her imagination, the abduction went something like this. She broke cover as Rachel was walking to her car. She threatened Rachel with the gun and forced her into the vehicle. There, she gagged her with duct tape and bound her hands with cable ties. Rachel would then be driven to a remote location and killed, her body hidden. Nobody would ever find her. It was, in Theresa's fevered brain, the perfect murder.

Except that it didn't work out that way. Rachel was not intimidated by the gun. Rather than submit, she took out her cell phone and dialed Brent. "That woman's here," was all she got to say before Theresa fired, hitting her in the chest. Brent heard the shots and the shouting but couldn't make out what was happening.

Neighbors, meanwhile, were dialing 911. A police cruiser was patrolling just a few blocks away and diverted to the address. The officer found Theresa Petto walking calmly down the road and arrested her. Two hundred yards away, Rachel Drafta was bleeding out in her driveway. Despite the swift response of paramedics, she would not make it. She died in the hospital two days later.

This was probably one of the easiest murder cases that Kalamazoo County prosecutors ever had to make. Not only was Theresa Petto arrested with the murder weapon in her hand but she was carrying a backpack that contained several rounds of .22 caliber ammunition, zip ties, rubber gloves, trash bags, and mace. There was also her journal, containing her detailed, point-by-point plan for the abduction and murder of her love rival, Rachel Drafto.

Faced with the overwhelming evidence against her, Theresa Petto had little option but to plead guilty at her September 2016 trial.

She did, however, cite mitigating circumstances, claiming that she was mentally impaired at the time of the shooting. This was ultimately rejected by the court. Petto was sentenced to life in prison. She is currently held at the Women's Huron Valley Correctional Facility in Ypsilanti. She will never be released.

Gunn-Britt Ashfield

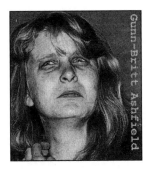

The small town of Nowra is a peaceful enclave situated on Australia's east coast. Located in an area of considerable natural beauty, it is a popular weekend destination for city dwellers traveling down from Sydney to enjoy the beautiful beaches, fine restaurants, and excellent local wineries. The area is also a haven for retirees seeking to escape the hustle and bustle of city life.

Brian and Gunn-Britt Ashfield were a long way from retirement age. They were, however, enjoying a life of relative leisure, living in government housing and subsisting on social security benefits. The pair were heavy drinkers and smokers and Brian had a history of drug abuse. Their other main interest appears to have been procreation. Still in their mid-twenties, they had five children, aged between three and eight years. That, as you might imagine, made for a rowdy household, something that Brian took in his stride but Gunn-Britt seemed to resent. She was frequently violent with her children, beating them mercilessly for the slightest

infraction. It was this penchant for child abuse that would
ultimately drive the couple apart.

In 1993, after yet another argument over Gunn-Britt's treatment of
the kids, Brian walked out. An uncontested divorce soon made the
separation official with Brian's pleas for custody ignored by the
court. He had a conviction for drug offenses and that counted
against him. The children were left in the dubious care of their
mother. Soon they'd have a stepfather, a local slacker named
Austin Hughes who, at 20 years of age, was five years younger
than Gunn-Britt.

Over the months that followed, social workers from the NSW
Department of Community Services made frequent visits to the
Ashfield residence, usually in response to complaints about the
treatment of the children. As many as 30 calls were logged and yet
the authorities refused to act, refused to remove the children from
their mother's custody, as Brian Ashfield was begging them to do.
Brian was seriously concerned about their welfare and he was
right to be anxious. Previously, it had been Gunn-Britt abusing the
children. Now, she had a more than willing accomplice – her new
boyfriend.

Of all the children, it was 6-year-old John who bore the brunt of his
mother's attention. The first-grader reminded Gunn-Britt of her
former husband and that alone seemed to warrant her wrath. The
poor child was mercilessly beaten, often without cause. He'd
frequently show up at East Nowra Primary School sporting fresh
bruises. Then a caseworker would be sent to interview Gunn-Britt
and would leave with assurances that the injury was accidental. It

was negligence bordering on dereliction of duty by the authorities. And it would come at a heavy price.

On the morning of August 5, 1993, Austin Hughes was in the children's bedroom when he spotted a pair of panties on the floor. The undergarment belonged to three-year-old Melissa and had a stain on it which Hughes assumed to be blood. He immediately called Gunn-Britt and showed her the panties. "John did this," he insisted. "He's been abusing his little sister." Although there was no proof that John had done any such thing, or even that any abuse had taken place, Gunn-Britt agreed. "He won't get away with this," she said. Then she and her boyfriend began planning an adequate punishment.

Six-year-old John Ashfield arrived home from school that day with no inkling of the storm he was walking into. He was barely through the door when he was accosted by this mother and dragged to the bedroom. "What have you done?" Gunn-Britt demanded, showing him the soiled panties.

"I haven't done anything," the little boy sobbed. Those denials fell on deaf ears. His mother and Ashley Hughes had each carried a weapon into the room. She had a thick telephone book; he had a claw hammer. Now they put these to use. Gunn-Britt pinned John to the bed by pressing the phone book down on the side of his head. Then Hughes started swinging with the hammer, pounding the book with as much strength as he could muster.

Standing in the doorway, John's siblings watched this horrific attack unfold. The two adults had now cast their weapons aside and were punching and kicking the child, ignoring his pleas for mercy. "You cry like a little girl," Hughes sneered. He then fetched a dress from the closet and forced it over John's head. While he was doing that Gunn-Britt removed the curtain rod from the rail and started beating her son, lashing his head, arms, and torso, striking with such force that the rod eventually bent. After one of those blows, John stopped screaming and lay still. He had been knocked unconscious.

It was at this point, with her rage finally dissipated, that Gunn-Britt realized that she might have gone too far. She started shaking John, trying to revive him, growing increasingly panicked as he failed to respond. She and Hughes dragged the child into the bathroom where they ran the shower on him, first cold and then scalding hot. Still, John showed no sign of life. His breathing was shallow, his pulse weak. His life, at this point, hung in the balance.

But still, Gunn-Britt failed to take action, failed to make the 000 call which would have brought the assistance that her son so clearly needed. Instead, she and Hughes sat down and concocted a cover story. Then, after warning the other children of the consequences if they told anyone what they'd seen, they loaded John into a car and drove him to the nearby Shoalhaven Hospital. There, doctors decided that he would have to be airlifted to Westmead Hospital in Sydney. Unfortunately, it was already too late. John's tiny body had suffered severe trauma. He was covered in over 100 bruises. He had several broken bones and he had sustained brain damage. Within 24 hours, he would be dead.

Interviewed by the police, Gunn-Britt and Hughes told an unlikely story. They said that John arrived from school battered and bruised and told them that he'd been attacked by bullies in a local park. He'd then collapsed into Gunn-Britt's arms. She and Hughes had then rushed him to the hospital. The police didn't believe this story for a minute but that did not stop Gunn-Britt from going on local television that night, to tearfully beseech the public to come forward with any information that would help bring her son's killers to justice.

Gunn-Britt had put on a convincing performance for the cameras. There can be few who saw that broadcast and did not feel her pain. By the following day, however, that sympathy had turned to revulsion. A search of the Ashfield residence turned up all the evidence that the police needed to confirm what they'd suspected all along. There was blood in the bedroom and on the bathroom tiles; there was a bent curtain rail encrusted with blood; there was a damaged phonebook with indentations that exactly matched a claw hammer that was found hidden under a bed. In no time at all, the killers were placed under arrest and led away in handcuffs.

With first-degree murder charges now hanging over their heads, the killers did what those of their ilk typically do in these circumstances – they turned on each other. Britt blamed Ashley and Ashley blamed Britt but their claims and counterclaims had little impact on the outcome of their case. Both were convicted and sentenced to 21 years in prison, sentences that were deemed far too lenient by most observers. There was an even bigger outcry when two years were knocked off on appeal. It seemed a scant price to pay for such a horrific crime.

FOOTNOTE:

Gunn-Britt Ashfield was released from Windsor John Maroney Prison in August 2011, having served 18 years of her 19-year sentence. Her parole conditions were stringent. She was required to wear a tracking device and would be subjected to frequent drug and alcohol screenings. Additionally, she was barred from contacting her children and was prohibited (at the family's request) from visiting John's grave. Ashley Hughes has also since been released. His whereabouts are unknown. As for Gunn-Britt, she is living under a new identity. With apparently no sense of irony, she changed her name to 'Angelic.'

Patricia Tito

Patricia Tito was a familiar sight in the bars and juke joints of Shreveport and Bossier City, Louisiana. A somewhat jaded blonde, now pushing on into her late thirties, she still knew how to work a room. And work it she did. She had a well-honed routine that usually involved zeroing in on any man who looked like he had a well-stocked wallet. The mark would be flattered and flirted into submission and would usually end up taking Patricia home. She'd then take up residence in his life, cadging and cajoling as much cash as she could before moving on to the next sucker. It wasn't prostitution exactly, but it was close.

The problem with Patricia's line of work was that her income was unpredictable. There were times of plenty and fallow periods during which she struggled to get by. At these times, she'd be forced to get a job and, being unqualified to do anything else, that usually meant waiting tables. This line of work was not without its benefits, though. There were plenty of male customers and

Patricia flirted shamelessly with every one of them. This typically got her a few extra bucks in tips but every once in a while, Patricia hit the jackpot. Like the day that 47-year-old Chris Shufflin walked into the diner where she was working.

Chris was a self-made man, a shrewd dealmaker in the oil industry. He worked for himself and he was good at what he did. Patricia noticed that right away by the way he dressed and by the thickness of his money clip as he peeled off some bills to pay for his meal. Before he left, she slipped him her phone number. Later that day, he called.

Meeting Chris wasn't just hitting the jackpot for Patricia, it was finding the pot of gold at the end of the rainbow. Her new beau was a big-hearted man and she tapped his generosity to the hilt. Almost daily, there were requests for cash and invariably these were met. In exchange, Chris got an experienced and adventurous lover, willing to indulge his every fantasy. It was an arrangement that held for a year until disaster struck. Chris suffered a stroke.

During the first few days of Chris's hospitalization, Patricia was a constant companion at his bedside, tearfully exhorting him to fight, to get better. But as Chris began to show signs of recovery, her emphasis changed. Now she was back to flirting and cajoling. She needed money to get her hair done and there was a pair of shoes that she just had to have. Could he write her a check or maybe give her his bank card and PIN? It was during this time, when he needed her support more than ever, that Chris finally saw the dark soul of the woman he'd fallen in love with.

Even so, Chris would probably still have accommodated Patricia's constant lust for cash. The problem was that the money wells had dried up. As a one-man operation, he only earned when he was out there, doing his thing. Right now, he was flat on his back and unable to work. Not only that but his hospital stay was costing him a lot of money, more than was covered by his health insurance. For the first time in the twelve months that they'd been together, he told Patricia no. Her response was to storm out of the hospital, expletives in her wake, never to return.

Recovering from a stroke is no small thing. But Chris Shufflin was as tough as they come. He was out of the hospital in record time and back to work long before doctors had recommended. He also moved on from Patricia and started dating a secretary named Judie Winn, who was ten years his senior. Judie was the polar opposite of his former lover. She was caring and refined and financially independent. Her interest was in Chris, not in his wallet.

While Chris was moving on with his life, Patricia had returned to her old stomping grounds. She was working the bars again, flirting, cadging drinks, trying to land her next meal ticket. But she'd been out of circulation for a while and most of her regular marks had either moved on or were wise to her scheme. Her fading looks, also meant that she had barely any luck with strangers. Eventually, she was left with only two options. It was either back to her waitressing gig or back to Chris. Unsurprisingly, she decided on the latter. An arrogant woman by nature, she was convinced that Chris would come running the moment she crooked her finger.

Unfortunately for Patricia, Chris had no interest in rekindling their romance. He told her that he was in a happy, committed relationship and asked her never to call him again. Then he hung up on her. That stung but what really hurt Patricia was what she found out about Chris's new girlfriend. Judie was 59 years old, 21 years older than she was. Had she really become so unattractive that she could lose out to a woman who was old enough to be her mother? A look in the mirror provided scant reassurance. Patricia's hard-drinking, hard-partying lifestyle had taken a toll. Her skin was sallow, her hair limp. There were wrinkles around her mouth, dark circles under her eyes.

It is typical of Patricia Tito's personality that her first thought was that Chris had left her because of her looks. It did not even enter her thinking that it was perhaps because she'd walked out on him when he'd needed her most. Still, Patricia was a determined woman. She believed that she could win Chris back and started inundating him with phone calls. When that didn't work she switched tactics and started leaving threatening messages on Chris's answering machine. Given what was to come, these make scary listening.

"You just better sleep with one motherf**king eye open," one message said. "Let me tell you something, partner. When I get ahold of Judie Winn, ain't nobody on God's green earth going to be able to make her f**king recognizable," another message went. "You have no idea what I'm going to do to the both of you," yet another said. "You'll never f**king see me coming. Do you hear me?"

Chris Shufflin and Judie Winn should probably have taken these threats seriously, should probably have reported them to the police. Sadly, they did not.

On the evening of August 31, 2003, Judie Winn hosted a dinner at her southeast Shreveport townhouse for Chris Shufflin and members of her family. Later, after her guests had left, and while Chris was in the bathroom, she was standing at the kitchen sink washing the dishes. She was so engrossed in her work that she did not even see Patricia Tito crossing the lawn towards her. When she looked up, Patricia was just feet away, standing on the patio, pointing a gun at her. Before Judie even had time to react, Patricia pulled the trigger, firing a single shot that passed through the open window and hit Judie in the chest.

By the time Chris reached his badly injured girlfriend, just moments later, Judie was lying on the kitchen floor, blood rapidly turning the front of her dress crimson. "Tricia Tito shot me," was all she managed to say before losing consciousness. Chris ran to the phone and dialed 911, bringing paramedics rushing to the scene. But it was already too late. For all of Chris's exhortations for her to hold on, Judy was just too badly injured. The bullet had chewed through vital organs and blood vessels, leaving carnage in its wake, causing irreparable damage. Judie never stood a chance.

Very little investigative work was needed to bring Patricia Tito to justice, not when the victim had named her as the shooter. She was arrested that same day and charged with first-degree murder.

Facing the possibility of life without parole, she decided to cop a plea to the lesser charge of manslaughter. The sentence of the court was 40 years in prison, with a stringent non-parole period of 38 years. Patricia Tito will be in her seventies by the time she is released from custody. Her days of trawling the bars for gullible men are well and truly over.

Tiana Browne

This is the story of two girls, teenage cousins growing up in the Crown Heights neighborhood of Brooklyn, New York in the mid-2000s. Yet the lives of 16-year-old Shannon Braithwaite and 15-year-old Tiana Browne could not have been more different. Shannon had been raised by her hardworking single mom, Marva. She was a pretty, outgoing girl who did well academically, enjoyed working with children, and loved dancing. She planned on attending college after high school and her mother had already set up a fund to make that happen. The future, for Shannon, was bright and assured. Tiana's future, by contrast, looked like a train wreck.

Tiana had been conceived out of wedlock when her mother was just 15 years old. She'd grown to be a moody, heavyset girl, raised by her grandmother and by the man who she came to regard as her step-grandfather. But when Tiana was in her mid-teens, she learned a dark and unsettling family secret. She found out that her step-grandfather was, in fact, her father, that he had raped her mother, and that she had been conceived as a result of that encounter. Her grandmother was apparently well aware of this. Tiana found it impossible to understand how the older woman could have remained with a man who had sexually assaulted and impregnated her teenage daughter.

The impact of this revelation was devastating to Tiana. She'd had her problems in the past but now she became almost uncontrollable, losing her temper at the slightest provocation, threatening violence, staying out late at night drinking and partying. On two occasions, she ran away from home and returned days later, battered and bruised, claiming that she had been raped. Unable to cope any longer, her grandmother turned to family and it was Marva, encouraged by her daughter Shannon, who agreed to take Tiana in. That would turn out to be a tragic mistake.

On the afternoon of Tuesday, September 30, 2008, just two days after Tiana moved into the Braithwaite residence, a 911 dispatcher received a call from a frantic young woman. She said that a man had broken into her home and murdered her cousin. The killer's name was Yusuf, she said, before hanging up. The police, of course, have protocols in place to trace hang-ups and they immediately started tracking this one, trying to locate the reported crime scene. They had not yet succeeded when there was another 911 call. Marva Braithwaite had arrived home to a sight no parent should ever see.

Shannon was lying on the kitchen floor in a pool of blood, her body perforated by multiple stab wounds, any number of which might have been fatal on its own. She was fully clothed except for her sneakers, which had been removed and were nowhere to be found. On the fridge, spelled out in magnetic letters, was the name "Yusuf," the man that the first caller had named as her cousin's killer. The police now knew the name of that caller – Tiana Browne.

But where was Tiana and what was her role in all this? Was she another victim of the mysterious Yusuf? Had she been abducted from the house? Had she been killed? The police didn't know yet. All they knew was that time was of the essence. The missing teen might be in danger. A search was launched immediately.

Tiana, as it turned out, was quite safe. She was tracked to a nearby park, where she was hanging out with her boyfriend. In her possession were her cousin's iPod, cell phone, and camera. She was also wearing Shannon's missing sneakers. Taken in for questioning, Tiana quickly admitted what the police already suspected. There was no Yusuf. It was she who had committed the brutal murder. According to Tiana, she'd acted in self-defense. Shannon had attacked her with a baseball bat and she had picked up a knife to protect herself.

But this story did not ring true. No bat was found in the home and defensive wounds on Shannon's hands suggested that she had tried to ward off the knife. Besides, Tiana had no injuries that would support her story of being struck with a bat. And what motive would Shannon have had for attacking her cousin? She was, by all accounts, a gentle and generous soul. It was she, after all, who had persuaded her mother to take Tiana in. The self-defense story was thus easily dismissed. Tiana was charged with first-degree murder. The decision was made to try her as an adult.

By the time the matter came to trial, Tiana Browne had expanded on her story. She was still claiming self-defense but now added that she'd blacked out during the attack and could not recall what had happened. Her lawyer had recruited a high-profile psychiatrist to back up the story. This expert testified that Tiana was suffering from Post-Traumatic Stress Disorder, the result of a traumatic childhood during which she'd been raped at age 13 and later gang-raped when she was 15 years old. Add to that the recent shock of having discovered the truth of her parentage and you have a human volcano, just waiting to blow. Tiana Browne, according to this expert, would have had no control over her actions.

The prosecution, of course, put its own witness on the stand and he was dismissive of the PTSD defense. The theory offered by the prosecutor was far simpler. Tiana was jealous of her cousin, jealous of her happy home life, her academic success, her looks, her prospects. She was jealous of the nice things that Shannon had, the electronic gadgets, the clothes, the new sneakers. She wanted these things for herself and so she murdered her cousin and took them. This was backed up by photos retrieved from Shannon's camera. Just hours after she so brutally ended her cousin's life, Tiana was captured on film, enjoying herself in the park with her boyfriend. It painted a picture of a callous young woman, one who was quite capable of killing to get what she wanted.

As the matter went to the jury, the odds appeared heavily stacked in favor of a conviction. Perhaps mindful of this, the defense asked that the jurors be allowed to consider manslaughter as a possible outcome. However, the judge refused. Tiana Browne would either be found guilty of murder or she would be acquitted on grounds of mental incapacity.

In the end, the outcome would frustrate both parties. During deliberations, it was discovered that the victim's mother, Marva Braithwaite, had a felony conviction for assault. She had not disclosed this during her testimony, leading the defense attorney to lodge a motion to dismiss, saying that he would have questioned her about her criminal record, had he known about it. It seemed a long shot but ultimately it was successful. Fearful of being overturned on appeal, the judge declared a mistrial.

And so to the second trial, beginning in July 2011. This was a far more straightforward affair that ended in a guilty verdict to a reduced charge of second-degree murder. Sentencing was scheduled for October. Before that, there were the witness impact statements and Marva Braithwaite's opportunity to address her niece directly. What she had to say brought many in the courtroom to tears.

"I took you in when no one else was prepared to help you," Ms. Braithwaite said. "You rewarded me by leaving me childless, ripping out my very being. When you sit behind bars, you can never say you weren't loved. Shannon loved you. I loved you. For the past three years, I have experienced more than the human mind can imagine. But there is no anger or bitterness in my heart. I want you to know that I forgive you for killing my daughter."

Tiana Browne was sentenced to 15 years to life. She could be free by her early thirties, the best part of her life still ahead of her. Her victim, Shannon Braithwaite, had not even lived to see her 17th birthday.

Zheng Yongshan

Zheng Yongshan was a rarity, a foreigner living in Japan. The Chinese national had moved to her adopted homeland in 2004 when she married a Japanese man. She already had a daughter by her husband but found it difficult to fit in. The Japanese are an insular people. They can be unwelcoming and suspicious of outsiders. Zheng would find that out first-hand during her first few years in the country.

Particularly stressful for Zheng were her interactions with the other young mothers at her daughter's school. Here, Japanese society is at its most cliquey. Every aspect of dress and behavior is scrutinized and evaluated, in both the child and the parent. If you make the cut, you're one of the in-crowd. If you do not, you're an outsider, cruelly and deliberately shunned.

Zheng, as a foreign national, never stood a chance. Her Japanese husband counted for nothing and neither did her adoption of the Japanese name, Mie Taniguchi. In the city of Nagahama, in the Shiga Prefecture, 300 km southwest of Tokyo, she and her daughter were on the outside looking in. Her only involvement with other parents was through the carpool she was a part of. On every third day, Zheng drove two other children, a little girl named Wakana Taketomo and a boy named Jin Sano, to kindergarten. The children were both five years old, the same age as Zheng's daughter.

It is easy to feel sympathy for Zheng Yongshan. All she wanted was to fit in, to be accepted for who she was. Yet nothing she did or said could gain her admittance to this exclusive club. When she took her daughter to the local park, the child was forced to play alone; when there were picnics or birthday parties, she was never invited. Zheng never received an invitation to the regular lunch parties that the other moms hosted either. And when they texted back and forth, gossiping and chatting, she was never on the list. It was an extremely isolating experience and over time it began to wear on her. Over time, she began to plot a terrible revenge.

On the morning of Friday, February 17, 2006, 34-year-old Zheng Yongshan rose early and got her daughter ready for school. This was one of those days on which Zheng was responsible for the carpool and so she stopped off at the Wakana and Jin residences to pick up her young charges, Sano and Taketomo. Then, with the children strapped into the back seat, she drove in the direction of the kindergarten. But this day would be different. Today, Zheng took a turn away from the school and drove away from the city center, towards the rice fields on its outskirts. When the children asked her about this, she said that they were going on an adventure.

But if this was an adventure, it was one fraught with mortal danger for the children. Zheng Yongshan was carrying in her car that day, a razor-sharp sashimi knife, one that she intended using. At a spot along a remote rural road, she brought the car to a stop and released her seatbelt. When she turned to face the perplexed five-year-olds, the knife was in her hand. She attacked without warning, stabbing and slashing with the 8-inch fish-filleting blade in a frenzy.

The children, trapped in place by their seatbelts, could do nothing to evade the onslaught. They were pierced in the stomach and the side, the narrow blade severing blood vessels and flaying organs. By the time their screams faded, Taketomo had been stabbed 19 times, Sano 13. With her traumatized daughter still buckled into the front seat, Zheng dragged the bodies from the car and dumped them at the side of the road. Then, she drove off.

A short while later, a farm worker was walking along the stretch of road when he made a horrific discovery, the blood-spattered body of a little girl. The man immediately raised the alarm and a blood trail soon led searchers to Jin Sano, who had dragged himself a short distance and was lying in an irrigation ditch. Both of the children were still alive and were rushed to a local hospital. However, their wounds were just too severe. The little girl, Taketomo, was dead on arrival. The boy, Sano, clung on until just before noon when he breathed his last. In the meantime, the children's red and pink schoolbags were found dumped beside another road. They would be shown in poignant footage on the evening's news bulletin.

From the very start, there was never any doubt as to who was responsible for the children's deaths. They had been in the custody of Zheng Yongshan and now Zheng was missing along with her daughter. As police launched a massive manhunt, Zheng's neighbors appeared before the TV cameras, telling reporters of her worrying behavior of late. They said that she had become increasingly bitter towards the other mothers at her daughter's school and had complained that her daughter was being bullied. No one, however, had expected that she'd go this far to get even.

Zheng Yongshan was found later that day, sitting in her parked car with her daughter, about 35 miles from the crime scene. She had made no attempt to conceal the evidence of the slaughter she had perpetrated. The back seat was still spattered with the blood of her victims and the bloody sashimi knife had been carelessly discarded on the floor. Taken into custody, she seemed barely aware of her surroundings. This disassociation from reality would form the basis of her legal defense.

Japan is a country with an exceedingly low crime rate. Yet, at the time that Zheng committed her atrocity, there had been an alarming spike in attacks on children under the age of 12. As many as 94 assaults were recorded over a nine-month period, many of them lethal. The most shocking of these was the mass killing of eight students, ranging in age from six to eight years, by a former psychiatric patient named Mamoru Takuma. Mamoru had been working at the school as a janitor when he went on a rampage with a butcher knife. He had been convicted and put to death in September 2004. Many expected the same for Zheng.

Zheng Yongshan went on trial at Otsu, the capital city of the Shiga Prefecture, in February of 2007, with the prosecution demanding the death penalty. Zheng's defense countered that she was mentally ill and called for a sentence commensurate with diminished responsibility if not an outright acquittal.

In the end, neither side got its way. After a defense-appointed psychiatrist testified that Zheng was suffering from schizophrenia, Judge Hidenori Nagai ruled that she was ineligible for the death penalty. However, the judge did not absolve her of responsibility, stating that she had formed a "strong intent to kill." He sentenced Zheng to life in prison. Both sides would later launch appeals against the sentence. Both were unsuccessful.

As for Zheng, she seems to have finally accepted responsibility for her deadly actions. She had launched her defense by callously claiming that "I stabbed sand dolls, not humans." By trial's end, though, she was singing a different tune. "I regret what happened," she told the court. "I'm sorry." That is scant consolation for two grieving families. It is no consolation at all for the two innocents whose young lives were so cruelly snatched away.

Lucy Cruz

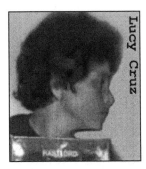

Lucy Cruz and Gloria Rivera were in love; deeply, passionately, hopelessly, in love. The pair had hooked up in 1990, in Hartford, Connecticut, and had soon moved into an apartment together. For Gloria, just 21 and somewhat inexperienced in the ways of the world, the flame burned particularly bright. This was her first serious relationship and she showed her devotion to her lover by having her name tattooed on her right buttock. She also gave Lucy an expensive gold necklace with the name "Gloria" etched on it. Lucy treasured this memento. At 35, she was more worldly than her girlfriend. Still, she'd never known a love quite like this one.

But here's the thing with intense, passionate relationships. They burn at a rate that is impossible to sustain. Eventually, one (or both) of the participants feels their desire waning, their attention drawn elsewhere. In this case, it was Gloria. Barely out of her teens, she was still ambivalent about her sexuality. She knew that she loved Lucy but also that she longed for something more. She wanted what her friends had. Some of them were already married. Some had children. Gloria was starting to see herself in the role of a wife and mother. It was a life that she could never have with Lucy.

A more mature individual might have sat Lucy down at this point, explained the dilemma, appealed to her better nature, let her down easy. But Gloria wasn't that person. Her approach was to begin staying out at night, partying with friends, sneaking in during the early morning hours. Usually, she'd get home to find Lucy waiting up for her, whatever the hour. Frequently, there were fights, with Lucy demanding an explanation and Gloria refusing to provide one. Lucy was convinced that her girlfriend was meeting up with men, an allegation that Gloria did not deny. This only added to Lucy's frustration. She became ever more controlling, even setting a midnight curfew for her lover. Gloria, of course, refused to abide by this restriction. Instead, she packed up her things and moved out. After three years, the relationship was over.

The breakup devastated Lucy and what made it even worse was that Gloria was still around. She'd moved in with friends in the same apartment building. That meant that Lucy saw her all the time and was constantly reminded of the love she'd lost. It was like twisting a knife in an open wound.

At first, Lucy was convinced that the separation was temporary, that Gloria would eventually come to her senses and return to her arms, that love would overcome. She sought to help this process along by cornering her ex at every opportunity, pleading with her to see reason. What they had was the real thing, she insisted, a one-in-a-lifetime thing. Although she couldn't promise marriage (the legalization of gay unions was still a couple of decades away), she did see a way for them to have children. They could adopt or Gloria could have in vitro fertilization. What Lucy didn't understand was that Gloria wasn't interested in a workaround. She wanted a traditional married life with a husband, a couple of kids, and a house in the suburbs.

Anyone who has ever been on the wrong side of a messy breakup can surely sympathize with Lucy Cruz. Yet, in even the most heartrending of separations, there comes a time when you have to let go. Lucy seems to have been incapable of doing so. Where sweet talk and persuasion had failed, she now resorted to intimidation. On one occasion she confronted Gloria in the hallway of their apartment block, drew a straight razor, and issued a stark warning. "I ever see you with a man and I'll kill both of you," she said. "And if you get pregnant, I'll cut the unborn baby right out of your belly." That unhinged rant should have been a stark warning to Gloria. Unfortunately, she failed to heed it.

On the night of September 3, 1993, Gloria was standing with a group of her friends in the parking lot of their building at 121 Bedford Street, when Lucy approached. She said that she needed to talk and ignored the group's urgings that she leave Gloria alone. Eventually, Gloria stepped forward to face her, at which point Lucy ripped the necklace that Gloria had given her from her neck, breaking it. She flung the broken chain at Gloria's feet, telling her that she was done and wouldn't be wasting any more time on her. Then she reached behind her into her waistband. When her hand came back, it was holding a small caliber pistol.

Two closely spaced shots were fired. At that range, it was impossible to miss. The .25-caliber bullets hit Gloria in the chest and dropped her to the tarmac, mortally wounded. Then, as Gloria lay bleeding on the tarmac, Lucy stood over her and spat, "That'll teach you!" Having delivered that rebuke, she turned and ran, got into her car, and sped away into the night. By the time first responders arrived, Gloria Rivera was already dead.

This was not a murder that Lucy Cruz was ever going to get away with. She had gunned down her ex in front of several witnesses, all of them more than willing to point her out as the killer. Still, Lucy managed to remain at large for nearly a week, while the police carried out a massive manhunt. In the interim, her family had hired a lawyer and it was he who persuaded her to give herself up. On September 10, 1993, the fugitive walked into a Hartford police station and informed the startled desk sergeant. "My name is Lucy Cruz. Apparently, I killed my girlfriend."

That declaration provided an insight into the defense that Cruz's lawyer, William Gerace, would put up at trial. According to Gerace, his client had suffered a mental breakdown and had gunned down Gloria Rivera in a fugue state. She could remember nothing of the actual shooting. She was unaware that anything had happened to Gloria until she saw the case profiled on television, with herself named as the perpetrator. The worst that she could be held responsible for was unintentional homicide.

Gerace put an expert witness on the stand to support his case. This eminent doctor testified that such psychotic episodes are not uncommon in these circumstances and that Lucy fit all of the criteria. Unfortunately for the defense, there were two glaring flaws with their argument. The first was that Lucy had gone into hiding immediately after the shooting. Why hide when you are not aware that you have done anything wrong?

The second flaw was contained within the final words that Lucy had spoken to the dying Gloria. Witnesses had heard her speak the words, "That'll teach you!" This suggests that the murder was an act of revenge, that it was deliberate, and that it had been planned. Those three spiteful words, spoken to the woman who had once been the center of Lucy Cruz's universe, would end up sinking the defense case.

Found guilty of murder, Lucy Cruz was sentenced to 35 years in prison. She was released on parole in 2017, having spent 23 years behind bars.

Dorothy Ellingson

It was the decade of decadence, the Roaring Twenties, the era of anything goes. Fueled by jazz music and a burgeoning trade in illegal booze, America was in party mood. Nowhere was that more true than in San Francisco.

But while the 1920s will go down in history as a time of relaxed moral standards, it was still an era when certain behaviors were frowned upon. Children, for example, were expected to obey their parents in all things, they were supposed to be seen and not heard, they were taught to be deferent and respectful to adults. Try telling that to Dorothy Ellingson.

Dorothy was a precocious 16-year-old who lived with her parents and older brother at 256 Third Avenue in the Inner Richmond area. Tall and flame-haired, she looked older than her years and acted way beyond them. Since her early teens, Dorothy's parents had endured endless disciplinary problems with her. She was quick to backchat, disposed to disobedience, impervious to discipline. She also got into trouble outside the home, skipping school and shoplifting. Already she'd had a couple of stints in juvenile hall but it had done nothing to mitigate her behavior. As Dorothy herself said, "There is something in my heart that makes me hate rules and regular hours. I like to do things when I feel like doing them or I don't want to do them at all."

Faced with their daughter's rebellious nature, Dorothy's parents tried different approaches to get through to her. While her father attempted to reason with the girl, her mother, Anna, was a disciplinarian. Dorothy was frequently grounded and given extra chores. She and her mother often engaged in furious shouting matches. Not that it made a jot of difference to Dorothy's behavior. If anything, her rebelliousness became more pronounced. It was almost as if she was making a point. She would not be tamed and would resist any attempt to dominate her.

And then things got even worse for Anna Elligson. When Dorothy was 15, she discovered jazz, the music that was sweeping the nation. In no time at all, she had obtained a fake ID, identifying her by the unlikely name of Montaine De Nero, aged 19. She used this to sneak into the illegal speakeasies that had sprung up all over the city. There she'd dance the night away, fueled by contraband rum and bathtub gin. It was also during this time that she became sexually active, an easy conquest for men twice her age or older. Since she was hardly discreet about her nocturnal activities, it did not take long before Anna found out.

Finding out about their teenager's sexual activity can be stressful for any parent, even in our supposedly enlightened times. Back then, when promiscuity was considered a mortal sin, it must have been devastating for Anna, more so because of the way that she found out. Dorothy kept a "little red book" in which she listed all of her conquests, rating their performance against various criteria and sparing none of the intimate details. This book came into Anna's possession after the police hauled Dorothy out of a speakeasy and forcibly brought her home. Reading the entries in the book, Anna was deeply shocked. "I went to Joe's party and met an amazing musician," one of the entries read. "He knows how to use all of his instruments."

Anna had now reached the end of her tether with Dorothy. She rounded on her daughter, launching a furious tirade in which she accused the teen of dragging the family's name through the mud. Then she threatened to have her placed in a reform school until she "came to her senses." Dorothy's response to this was to run away from home, following a jazz musician to Los Angeles. Again, it was the police who tracked her down and brought her back to her long-suffering parents.

If the relationship between mother and daughter had been bad before Dorothy's flight to L.A., it got even worse now. Previously, the battle had been confined to verbal sparring. Now, it got physical. Anna and Dorothy frequently had to be separated as they slapped and clawed and wrestled with each other. Familial relations reached their nadir on the night of January 13, 1925, when Dorothy tried to leave the apartment and Anna physically stopped her from doing so. The two women ended up rolling around on the floor in an unseemly fight. In the end, Anna won out. Her victory, though, would come at a high price.

Prevented from going out on that January evening, Dorothy spent the night fuming in her bedroom. She slept hardly a wink and instead lay plotting revenge against her mother. Eventually, she heard the household coming to life, her mother getting up to prepare breakfast, her father and brother going through their morning routines and then leaving for work. Finally, it was just her and her mother in the house. That was when Dorothy rose from her bed, snuck into her brother's bedroom and fetched the revolver that he kept hidden there. Carrying the weapon with her, she walked down to the kitchen, where her mother was standing at the sink, washing the dishes. With her back turned, Anna did not see Dorothy raise the revolver and take aim. Two shots were fired at close range, both of which struck Anna in the back of the head. She was dead by the time she slumped to the floor.

So what did the 16-year-old murderess do now that she had killed her mother? Did she call the police? Did she confess her guilt and claim provocation? Did she concoct some cover story? None of the above. Dorothy Ellingson simply packed her best frocks into a suitcase, raided the apartment for her mother's housekeeping money, and then left. She spent that night dancing at a local speakeasy, partying into the early morning hours.

Of course, the body had already been discovered by now. Dorothy's brother, Earl, found it when he returned from work. Earl then called the police who surmised from the scene that an intruder had broken in and killed Anna. But Earl and his father offered a different theory. They suspected Dorothy. After determining that some of the girl's clothing was missing, the police reluctantly drew the same conclusion and launched a search. Dorothy was found a few days later, living with one of her girlfriends. She made no attempt to deny responsibility for her mother's murder. Asked why she had done it, she issued the infamous reply: "She scolded me."

The case of the murderous "jazz baby" soon became a media sensation, not just in the Bay area but across the nation. Matricide was an extremely rare crime in those days. There were many who simply refused to believe that a 16-year-old girl would kill her own mother. Even District Attorney Mathew Brady was dumbfounded. "Not in the history of California crime have I found a case where a daughter killed her mother," Brady told the media. "I know of no case where a minor has been guilty of this crime."

One theory doing the rounds at the time was that someone else had shot Anna and that Dorothy was covering for the real killer. Another, favored by various church leaders, was that jazz music was to blame. "Jazz goes back to the African jungle and its effect is to make you want to go on all-fours and whisk your tail around a tree," a prominent Episcopal bishop asserted. From then on a new term entered the common parlance – jazz mania. Exposure to this music could induce a form of hysteria that relieved you of your morality, the theory went. This, of course, played right into the hands of Dorothy's lawyers who declared their intention of pleading her insane.

At the trial, Dorothy Ellingson played right into the insanity narrative. She fainted on numerous occasions and at times appeared catatonic and had to be carried from the courtroom. At other times, she raged against the prosecuting attorney and even screamed at her lawyer. And the histrionics worked...to a degree. Rather than being convicted of murder, she was found guilty of manslaughter. The sentence of the court was ten years. She would end up doing seven.

While serving her time, Dorothy gave several interviews renouncing her old life and urging children to respect their parents and stay in school. After her release in 1932, she lived for a time with her father, who had apparently forgiven her for killing his wife. However, for all the talk of rehabilitation, Dorothy was still a rule breaker by nature. In 1933, less than a year after her release, she was arrested for stealing $600 in cash, clothes, and jewelry from her roommate. Surprisingly, given her prior record, she received only probation for this offense.

Dorothy (now using the name Diane Jentoff) next shows up on our radar in 1936, when she married a construction worker named Robert Stafford. She would bear him two children, a boy and a girl, before that familiar restlessness overwhelmed her and she walked out on the marriage. In 1955, as Diane Stafford, she was arrested for stealing $2,000 worth of jewelry from her employer. Brought to the Marin County jail, Dorothy was confronted by a familiar face in the adjacent cell. Her 17-year-old son had just been hauled in on a charge of burglary. The apple, it seemed, had not fallen far from the tree.

Dorothy Ellingson died on September 16, 1968. She was 59 years old.

Sarah "Cindy" White

On the night of December 31, 1975, a deadly fire broke out in a residence in Greenwood, Indiana. Seven souls were inside the house at the time – a forty-something couple named Charles and Carole Roberson; their four young children, aged between four and seven years; and the children's live-in nanny, 18-year-old Sarah White, known to all as Cindy. Only the nanny made it out alive. She'd soon find herself charged with six counts of murder.

The story of Cindy White has a tragic genesis that is all too common in cases involving young offenders. Cindy was born in Greenwood in 1957, one of six children. Her mother was an alcoholic, her father a sexual predator who targeted Cindy from the time she was just nine years of age. This abuse continued throughout her teens and resulted eventually in a mental breakdown.

One morning in 1973, Cindy woke to find that she was unable to move her legs. She was transported to a nearby hospital where doctors could find nothing physically wrong with her. They suspected that her problem might be mental and referred her to a psychiatric facility in Indianapolis. Here, experts confirmed the diagnosis. The trauma she'd suffered had caused Cindy's brain to stop sending signals to her legs.

Cindy would spend ten months as an in-patient at the psychiatric hospital. During that time, she attended regular counseling sessions but never once revealed the abuse she'd suffered at her father's hands. The shame of it weighed too heavily on her. Like many victims of sexual exploitation, she placed much of the blame on herself. Nonetheless, she gradually recovered the use of her legs. Eventually, she was ready to go home. That was a problem. Home meant cohabitating with her father again. Cindy wasn't about to do that.

It is at this point in the story that Charles and Carole Roberson stepped in to throw Cindy White a lifeline. It is unclear how Cindy knew the Robersons although it has been suggested that she'd met them while working a newspaper route as a teenager. In any case, she knew them to be a friendly couple who had always been nice to her. When they offered her a job as a live-in nanny to their four young children, she jumped at the chance.

Life with the Roberson family was a blessing to Cindy, at least in the beginning. The kids were rambunctious but a joy to be around; the adults were kind and caring. But then one day, while Carole was out of the house, Charles invited her into his bedroom. What followed wasn't forced upon her. Carole gave herself willingly but she wasn't really in a fit mental state to give consent. She was an abused teen, still nursing unhealed mental scars from her childhood. That vulnerability was exploited by the older man. Cindy had traded one abuser for another.

Still, Cindy believed herself to be in love with Charles Roberson. The two of them began exchanging love notes and sneaking around behind Carole's back. At least, that was what Cindy believed at the start. Then, one night while she was in bed with Charles, Carole walked into the room and disrobed, joining them in a threesome. Thereafter, this would become a routine. Charles also started bringing a camera into the bedroom to take snapshots of the action. Cindy, who'd gotten into this believing that Charles was in love with her, realized now that she was being used, exploited as a sexual plaything.

Later, once the dust had settled and six people were dead, the question would be asked of Cindy, "Why didn't you just leave?" The answer that she offered is impossible to verify. For what it's worth, Cindy claimed that Charles threatened her, promising that he'd hunt her down and kill her if she ever ran out on him. If that is true, then that threat contained in it the seeds of a tragedy.

For Cindy was desperate to leave, frantic to escape her current situation. And if simply walking away was not an option, she needed another plan. In December 1975, a solution presented itself. One of Cindy's sisters called to let her know that there had been a fire at their grandmother's house. Everyone had escaped unharmed but the house had been gutted by the blaze and rendered unlivable. That was when the idea first occurred to Cindy. If the Robersons' house were to be similarly damaged, they'd be forced to let her go.

On New Year's Eve 1975, with the Roberson family all abed, Cindy White put her plan into action. Rising from the couch where she made her bed at night, she walked to the kitchen and fetched some newspaper. She scrunched several sheets into tight balls, then rammed these into the sides of Charles's favorite recliner. Then she lit a match and applied it to a corner of the paper. Flames immediately caught hold and danced before her eyes. Then another piece of her kindling started to smolder, then another. Suddenly, the entire chair was ablaze. Then the flames spread to the adjacent Christmas tree. Cindy had expected a slow burn. What she got instead was an instant inferno.

This had been a serious miscalculation. Cindy realized that now. Running down the hall, she started banging on doors, trying to rouse the sleeping family. From within the master bedroom, Carole responded with a series of hacking coughs, telling her to run out into the yard and to wait by the kitchen window so that she could pass the children through. Cindy did as she was told but Carole never made it to the window. The flames and the smoke had now taken control of the house. As Cindy tried to re-enter the building, a neighbor appeared and dragged her away. "I have to get to the children!" she shouted at her would-be rescuer. "It's too late," was his response.

As the only survivor of the deadly fire, Cindy White immediately came under suspicion. Her story, that the Christmas tree had spontaneously burst into flames, just didn't ring true. Once fire inspectors found clear evidence of arson, she was taken into custody. Then detectives searched the wreckage of the house and found love letters, written by Cindy to Charles, and also nude photos of Cindy. That gave them a possible motive for murder. The theory was that Cindy had been in love with her employer and that he had ended the affair, leaving her angry and set on revenge. She'd wiped out his entire family to express her rage.

That, in any case, was the hypothesis offered by the prosecution at trial. Cindy's defense was still arguing that this was just a tragic accident but, in the end, the jury ruled against her. Convicted on six charges of capital murder, Cindy White was sentenced to six life terms without parole. She also received a twenty-year term for arson. Given the length of her primary sentences, that was entirely academic.

In 1986, ten years after she began serving her sentence, Cindy White eventually came clean and admitted that she had deliberately started the deadly fire. She denied, however, that she'd acted with malice, insisting that she had loved the children and would never have hurt them intentionally. At this time, White also talked about the abuse she'd suffered, first by her father and then by Charles and Carole Roberson. It made no difference to her sentence. She remains behind bars. Save for an intervention by the governor, she will die there.

Beatrice Cenci

It reads like a novel by Umberto Eco, a dark, medieval drama involving familial violence, incest, torture, and cold-blooded murder. But the story of Beatrice Cenci is true, tragically so. Beatrice was a beautiful, young noblewoman, living in Rome during the late 1500s. She was the daughter of Count Francesco Cenci, a man with a terrible reputation. Francesco had inherited his title, and his great fortune, from his father, Cristoforo. He, in turn, had acquired much of his wealth through embezzlement, extortion, and other criminal activities. And the apple did not fall far from the tree. Francesco Cenci was, by all accounts, a dreadful human being.

Francesco's anti-social behavior could be traced back to his youth when he was a frequenter of brothels, a seducer of young women, and a ferocious street brawler who often attacked innocent passersby just for the hell of it. He was also unspeakably cruel and sexually violent towards servants in his father's household. And

his behavior did not improve once he inherited the Cenci fortune.
Now, his preferred crime was defrauding creditors, something that
frequently landed him before the courts and sometimes in the
cells. On each of these occasions, he was freed after paying a small
fine. Cenci's abhorrent behavior wasn't restricted to strangers
either. Three of his sons were left destitute by his refusal to
support them financially. They eventually had to obtain a papal
decree to obtain a settlement.

By 1594, however, Count Cenci's profligate ways were finally
beginning to catch up with him. A long-running dispute with the
Catholic Church, over monies that his father had reportedly
embezzled from the papal coffers, was coming to the boil; the cries
of cheated creditors were becoming ever more strident; he was
fretting over the payment of a dowry for the upcoming marriage of
his daughter, Antonina. In the midst of all this, Cenci was accused,
and then convicted, of sodomizing one of his servants. This was a
serious offense, one that carried the death penalty. He would
almost certainly have been burned at the stake had he not agreed
to forfeit one-third of his estate to the Roman government.

Francesco Cenci was an inherently tightfisted man, so the loss of
such a considerable fortune hurt him deeply. Over the next three
years, he continued to rant against the injustice of his sentence. In
his worst moments, he even suggested that he'd have been better
off refusing the fine and submitting to execution. Finally, in 1597,
he decided that he was going to remove himself from Rome. His
family owned a castle at Petrella, a foreboding structure perched
high on a crag in the Kingdom of Naples, just beyond the borders
of the Papal States. This would keep him out of the reach of the
Roman authorities and of his increasingly strident creditors.

Accompanying Francisco on his retreat (and given no choice in the matter) were his second wife, Lucrezia, his daughter Beatrice, and his stepson, Bernardino, a boy of twelve. And they would soon learn that they were not guests at the castle but prisoners. The traveling party had barely arrived when Francisco ordered the windows in the rooms of his wife and daughter to be bricked up. Complaints regarding this injustice were met with swift and violent retribution. So too were any other infractions. Lucrezia was thrashed with a riding crop when she dared reprimand Francisco for an attempted sexual assault on her young son; Beatrice was flayed with a bullwhip when the master of the house learned that she had been in contact with her older brother, Giacomo.

The letter to Giacomo carried a simple message... "Help!" In it, Beatrice claimed that her father was keeping her locked up out of stinginess. He did not want her to find a husband because he was too mean to stump up for another dowry. Beatrice also made another, far more serious, allegation. She said that her father had been visiting her bedroom at night and forcing himself on her.

This allegation would later be the foundation of a self-defense claim at Beatrice's trial. We can't say for certain whether it is true but it is certainly believable, given the character of the man we're dealing with. Beatrice, as we have already noted, was a renowned beauty. Petite and pretty, she looked a lot younger than her 23 years. That would have appealed to a pedophile like Francesco. It is not a stretch to imagine that he might have broken the ultimate taboo and raped his daughter.

Giacomo, in any case, was outraged by the allegation. He had his
own (mostly financial) reasons to hate his father. Now he sprang
into action, roping his sister and stepmother into a murder
conspiracy. Also recruited into the plot was Olimpio Calvetti, the
keeper of the Castello La Petrella. He had his own reason for
wanting his master dead. He had fallen in love with Beatrice.
Giacomo who, along with Beatrice, was the main author of the plot,
was uninvolved other than to give his consent and to supply the
conspirators with a vial of antimony. In the end, the idea of using
poison was abandoned. Francisco was suspicious to the point of
paranoia. If he had any inkling that something was amiss, the game
would be up.

And so, a Plan B was derived. This involved Olimpio Calvetti
entering the master's chamber by night and bludgeoning him to
death in his sleep. September 9, 1598, was chosen as the night for
the murder. When the hour arrived, Lucrezia wavered and had to
be persuaded by her stepdaughter, Beatrice. Lucrezia then
unlocked the door to her husband's bedroom and Olimpio entered,
accompanied by a local tinker named Marzio Catalano, who he had
recruited. Francesco was struck repeatedly on the head with a
hammer and died without waking. His body was then dragged out
and tossed from a balcony, to make it appear that he had suffered
an accidental fall.

This was not a particularly well-conceived murder. But in an age
when there was no formal police force and certainly no detectives,
the conspirators should have gotten away with it. In fact, members
of the Cenci family all but assured this when they had Olimpio

Calvetti murdered, to assure that he would never be able to talk. Unfortunately, they forgot about Marzio Catalano, Olimpio's accomplice. The tinker was also somewhat of a traveling minstrel and was seen in several villages wearing a particularly fine cloak, a garment he'd taken in payment for his participation. This attracted the attention of the authorities and he was arrested. The interrogation tactics of the day involved torture so it is no surprise that Marzio soon spilled the beans, naming his illustrious cohorts.

Taken into custody, Giacomo, Lucrezia, and Beatrice all initially denied involvement. But a few rounds with a skilled torturer and they were talking, turning on each other. Giacomo and Lucrezia named Beatrice as the mastermind and prime mover. Beatrice, in turn, blamed her dead lover, Olimpio. These denials did none of them any good. Placed on trial (together with 12-year-old Bernardino who does not appear to have played any part in the plot) they were all convicted and sentenced to death.

The sentences caused uproar among the common people of Rome, who took to the streets in protest. Petitions were also submitted to Pope Clement VIII, begging for clemency. The Pope, who was no friend of Francisco Cenci, might well have interceded. But he was dealing with another high-profile familial murder at that time - the Countess of Santa Croce had recently been killed by her son for financial gain. Fearing a spate of such crimes, the Pope decided only to commute the sentence of young Bernardino. The other conspirators would be put to death.

Roman executions in those days were carried out in public at the Ponte Sant'Angelo, a bridge spanning the Tiber. At dawn, on

September 11, 1599, the three condemned persons were loaded onto a cart and brought to their place of dying. Giacomo Cenci's death was particularly brutal. He was subjected to horrible torture on his last ride and arrived at the scaffold in a barely conscious state. There, his skull was smashed with a mallet and his body was then quartered. Lucrezia and Beatrice, standing in the cart, would have seen all of this before their deaths, as would 12-year-old Bernardino, who was forced to watch the executions. For Lucrezia and Beatrice, this was done by beheading with a sword. Lucretia went first, then Beatrice, insisting to the end that the murder of her father was justified, given his vile abuse.

Another consequence of Francisco Cenci's murder was the confiscation of all the Cenci properties. In theory, these should have been forfeited to the Roman state. In practice, they were scooped up by Pope Clement's family, leaving the rightful heir, Bernardino Cenci, destitute. Bernardino had been sentenced to serve out his life as a galley slave but was reprieved after a year. Now he was free to live up to the Cenci name, which means "rags" in Latin.

But the real legacy of this tragic story belongs to Beatrice. She was buried in the church of San Pietro in Montorio, her funeral attracting a massive crowd. In the years to come, she would be held as a symbol of the common people, against the tyranny of the aristocratic class. Legend has it that her ghost appears on the Ponte Sant'Angelo every year on the anniversary of her death, carrying her severed head in its hands.

Geraldine Smith

In 1985, in Chicago, Illinois, factory workers Geraldine Smith and Louia McDonald were caught up in a torrid love affair. The problem with this liaison, as is so often the case, was that the lovers had different views on what their relationship meant. To Louia, a married man with two young daughters, it was about sex, pure and simple. To Geraldine, it was something far deeper. She was in love with Louia and wanted to be with him. Louia, willing to do anything to have his way, told her that he was working on it. In the manner of cheating men the world over, he claimed that his wife didn't understand him, that he was unhappy at home, that he was only hanging in there for the sake of his kids.

In truth, Louia McDonald's home life was far from unhappy. He was quite content with his wife of seventeen years and had no intention of leaving her. The fact of the matter was that Louia wanted to have his cake and eat it too. And so, he continued stringing his lover along, making and breaking promises, while

Geraldine clung desperately to hope. Eventually, as Louia continued to stall, she resorted to desperate measures and stopped using birth control. In early 1986, she informed Louia that she was pregnant with his child. If that was intended to force his hand, it had to opposite effect.

Geraldine Smith had just learned a painful lesson. Married men seldom leave their wives for a mistress. When the chips are down, they almost always return home. This is precisely what Louia did, even admitting to his wife, Valerie, that he'd been unfaithful. Valerie, a staunch Christian who was devoted to her husband and children, forgave him. The couple got to work patching up their relationship. It would have ended right there if Geraldine had been prepared to move on. Geraldine was not going to do any such thing.

In June 1986, an obviously pregnant Geraldine confronted Valerie McDonald on the street outside her apartment, unleashing a torrent of abuse at the startled woman. Valerie tried to calm her down but that only served to enrage Geraldine. She attacked suddenly, slapping and punching, knocking Valerie to the ground. It was at that moment that a police cruiser pulled up. Geraldine was restrained and led away in handcuffs, still spitting and cursing. A search of her car turned up a fully loaded .25 caliber pistol. This could have ended far worse.

Geraldine was booked on common assault. Three months later, in October of 1986, she gave birth to a healthy baby boy. Seeking to make a point, she named the child Louia McDonald Jr. But if this was meant to curry favor with the baby's father, it failed dismally. After an initial visit to see his son, Louia stopped coming around.

This was callous, unforgivable behavior by Louia McDonald. He'd used Geraldine Smith, made promises he had never intended keeping, broken those promises. Now, in her hour of need, he'd cast her aside, abandoned her as though she'd never meant a thing to him. Hurt and humiliated, Geraldine would have been more than justified in any hostility she felt towards him. No one would have blamed her. But Geraldine's anger wasn't directed at the man who had betrayed her but rather at the innocent party in all of this. In her mind, it was Valerie who was the impediment to her happiness. If only Valerie were out of the picture, then she and Louia could be together, happily ever after.

Geraldine was making just this point to her friend Marva Golden, one day in June 1987. "That bitch needs to die," she spat and Marva sympathized, saying that she knew how Geraldine felt. From there, the conversation quickly devolved to darker tones, to the idea of actually killing Valerie McDonald. Geraldine said that she'd give five one-hundred dollar bills to anyone who could make it happen. Marva responded that she knew a man who'd take her money.

The cut-rate assassin that Marva had in mind was a lowlife named Eddie Williams, 29 years of age, with about half of those years spent incarcerated in some or other correctional facility. A meeting was arranged at which Geraldine peeled off the five bills that would pay to end a woman's life. Four of those bills were pocketed by Williams. The other went to Marva Golden as a finder's fee. Geraldine also provided her car as a getaway vehicle and her .25 caliber handgun to carry out the shooting. The date was set. Valerie would die on June 23, 1987.

Here's the thing about criminal conspiracies. They are usually poorly conceived by hair-brained individuals who think that they're smarter than they are. This one was no different. On the night in question, Geraldine took her son to visit family, thus ensuring that she had an alibi. Marva and Eddie Williams drove in Geraldine's car to the Belmont area of Chicago. There, Marva pulled onto a side street and Williams got out and walked towards an apartment building on Winthrop Avenue, where he took up a position in the darkness. At this precise moment, Louia McDonald was picking up his wife and daughters from a church meeting, driving them home, bringing them directly into the shooter's arc of fire.

The McDonald family arrived at their apartment block just before 10 p.m. on that Tuesday evening. They were about to enter the building when a man stepped out from the shadows. No one saw the gun in his hand until he raised it, pointed it at Valerie, and then discharged a single bullet into her head. As Valerie collapsed to the ground in front of her stunned daughters, the man took off running, with Louia in close pursuit. Unfortunately, (or perhaps fortunately) the shooter was too fast for him. Louia arrived just in time to see the man getting into a burgundy-colored car, which then raced away in a squeal of tires. Louia knew that vehicle well. It belonged to Geraldine Smith.

Valerie McDonald wasn't killed outright by the bullet. She would linger in a coma for six days before she eventually passed, without ever regaining consciousness. By then, her killers were already in custody. Geraldine Smith had been arrested after Louia revealed that the killer had used her car to make his getaway. Questioned by detectives, Geraldine insisted that she'd had nothing to do with the shooting. According to her, she'd loaned the vehicle to her friend Marva Golden for the night. She suggested that the police speak to Marva, which they were happy to do. Then, after examining Geraldine's car, they picked up Eddie Williams' prints on a side window and brought him in. Within just 48 hours of the shooting, all three of the conspirators were in police custody.

Geraldine Smith would prove the hardest nut for the police to crack. She continued to protest her innocence even as the evidence piled up against her. It was her gun that had been used in the shooting, her car that had facilitated the getaway. Even more importantly, it was she who had motive, whereas the other suspects did not. But the police did not need Geraldine's cooperation, not when her cohorts were so willing to talk. Williams and Golden soon confessed to their involvement, naming Geraldine as their "client." Perhaps the most shocking revelation was the price that had been paid for the hit. The life of a good, churchgoing woman, of a devoted mother-of-two, was worth just $500.

Marva Golden and Eddie Williams entered guilty pleas at their respective trials, earning terms of 20 years and life in prison respectively. Geraldine Smith decided to take her chances with a jury but was nonetheless convicted of first-degree murder and conspiracy to commit murder. She was condemned to death, although the sentence was later commuted to life in prison. The cold-hearted killer would spend just 17 years behind bars before her release in 2008. Louia McDonald, whose selfish, duplicitous behavior had set this tragedy in motion, has only his conscience to answer to.

Jean Sinclair

To the residents of the retirement home that she operated in Salt Lake City, Utah, Jean Sinclair was known as, "The King." It wasn't that she was a tyrant or anything. Quite the opposite. Jean was a shrewd businesswoman who knew that the happiness of her clients was paramount to her success. Her regal epithet came from the fact that Jean was a Type A personality, someone who wanted things done just so and always got her way. But why "The King" rather than "The Queen"? That would have to do with another quirk of Jean's character. She liked dressing in men's suits and her mannerisms were decidedly masculine. In an era when same-sex relationships were still criminalized in the United States, Jean Sinclair was unapologetic about her attraction to women.

One woman, in particular, held Jean's attention. She was a 26-year-old divorcee named LaRae Peterson, who worked at the rest home as the in-house beautician. Petite, demure, and quite pretty, LaRae caught Jean's eye from day one. She began showering her

employee with attention, buying her gifts, helping her out
financially. By 1957, the two of them were involved in a steamy
affair, sneaking off to motels for their illicit trysts. Over the next six
years, the relationship deepened. For Jean, at least, it was true
love. She believed that she'd found her soulmate.

LeRae, though, was not as committed to her alternative lifestyle.
Much as she loved Jean, she still hankered after the life she'd left
behind. She still believed that Mr. Right was out there, waiting to
sweep her off her feet and into his strong arms. She still yearned to
be a wife and a mother. And so, LeRae started dating in secret,
seeing men behind Jean's back. That was how she met Don Foster.

Don was exactly the kind of man that LeRae had dreamed of. Six-
foot-tall and handsome with it, he had an easygoing nature and an
old-school charm that women found irresistible. LeRae was
certainly taken with him. When, after just a few weeks of dating,
Don proposed marriage, she accepted in a heartbeat. It was only
later that evening that an ominous truth dawned on her. Jean was
not going to take this well. Breaking the news to her was
something that filled LeRae with dread.

As it turned out, LeRae would be relieved of the burden of
revelation. Jean found out before LeRae ever had the chance to
admit to her indiscretion. That sparked an angry exchange
between the lovers during which Jean stormed off, telling LeRae
that she wished she'd never met her. Later, she would retract that
statement, penning a tearful letter in which she begged LeRae for
another chance. "I don't care who you see when we're not

together," she wrote. "Just don't cut me out of your life. I can't live without you."

Unfortunately for Jean, LeRae's mind was already made up. She was tired of sneaking around, drained by the need for secrecy, weary of the threat of arrest and the public humiliation that would bring. She was moving on with her life and begged Jean to do the same.

This, however, was not a scenario that Jean was prepared to even contemplate. To her, the idea that LeRae might love someone else just didn't make sense. Quite obviously, Don had beguiled her in some way. Thus, the solution was obvious. Remove Don from the equation and LeRae would come running back to her. She was convinced of it.

And so, Jean started brainstorming, trying to figure out a way to get rid of her love rival. Some of her ideas were quite outlandish. For example, she proposed to a couple of associates, Vaughn Humphries and Karl Kuehne, that they should kidnap Don and castrate him. When her cohorts balked at this idea, she suggested that they could just hold a knife to his testicles and threaten him with castration unless he ended things with LeRae and left town. Then she had another idea. She proposed that they drug LeRae and force her to perform a lesbian act, making Don watch. This, she hoped, would "put him off" LeRae. Again Humphries and Kuehne said no. They were both ex-cons and had no desire to return to the penitentiary.

By the fall of 1962, Jean's stance against Don Foster had hardened considerably. She frequently ranted about him, once telling Kuehne, "I think that son-of-a-bitch ought to be killed." In December of 1962, she persuaded Kuehne to buy her a shotgun and a box of shells, saying that she planned to do some pheasant hunting. Given her bile-filled tirades against Don Foster, Kuehne should have been suspicious of this request. But no one refused "The King" and so Kuehne complied. He even sawed down the shotgun barrel when Jean asked him to.

On the afternoon of January 5, 1963, LeRae Peterson received an unexpected call from her former lover. Their last few exchanges had been less than civil and so LeRae was somewhat surprised by Jean's friendly demeanor. She was all sweetness and light, saying how much she regretted her prior behavior. She then suggested that the three of them might get together for a drink so that she could make her apologies in person. LeRae thanked her for the invitation but said that she and Don already had plans for dinner and a movie that night. Jean appeared to take this in good grace. "Some other time then," she said as she hung up the phone.

LaRae Peterson could not have known it but she had just made a fatal error. She had just revealed to a deeply unstable woman, her plans for the evening. When she and Don arrived back at the Susan Kay Arms apartment complex that night, Jean Sinclair was waiting, crouching in the shadows among the parked vehicles, clutching her sawn-off shotgun. When Don got out of the car and rounded the vehicle to open the door for LeRae, Jean stepped from cover. Without uttering a sound, she raised the weapon and fired, catching Don full in the face with a lethal spray of pellets.

At that short distance, Don never stood a chance. He was flung
back by the blast, thrown to the blacktop even as Jean turned and
fled the scene. LeRae, emerging from the vehicle, saw her fiancé on
the ground, his face reduced to bloody hamburger. Her anguished
screams rebounded off the surrounding buildings. "She killed him.
Oh my God, she killed him."

Don Foster was taken to a Salt Lake City hospital, where he was
pronounced dead on arrival. By then, the police had already
identified a suspect. Several witnesses had reported a man fleeing
the scene in a light-colored sedan. LeRae assured them that it
wasn't a man but a woman who liked to dress in men's clothing.
Jean Sinclair was arrested that same night. Despite her insistence
that she'd been in the company of her brother and sister-in-law all
evening, she was charged with murder.

With its revelations of lesbian lust, venomous jealousy, and cold-
blooded murder, this was one of the most sensational cases of the
era. Jean Sinclair entered a not guilty plea at trial and the defense
put her brother and sister-in-law in the witness box to provide her
with an alibi. But that was never likely to be accepted by the all-
male jury. Karl Kuehne's testimony, in particular, was devastating
to Jean's case. After he told the court about buying the gun, about
sawing it down, about Sinclair's hatred for the victim, her fate was
all but sealed. Still, it took the jury a full seventeen hours to reach
its verdict. Jean's only consolation was that it came with a
recommendation of mercy. But for that, she would likely have
ended up on death row.

Jean Sinclair entered the Utah State prison system in April 1964, a
life sentence stretching out ahead of her. In her case, life would
mean less than ten years. In 1973, Sinclair suffered a stroke while
being held at the Weber County Jail. As a result, the Utah Board of
Pardons granted a parole on medical grounds and placed her in a
rest home. She passed there, months later, at the age of just 55. Up
until the day she died, she continued to insist that she was
innocent of the murder of Don Foster.

But those protestations are almost certainly a lie. No one but
Sinclair had motive, no one but she knew the approximate time
that Don and LeRae were expected home. Factor in the purchase of
the murder weapon, just days before the shooting, and the case
more or less makes itself.

It is an entirely circumstantial case, though, and that always leaves
room for reasonable doubt. In another place, another time, Jean
Sinclair might well have been acquitted. Perhaps there is some
merit to the claims of Sumner J. Hatch, Sinclair's defense attorney.
He insists that his client was not convicted for killing Don Foster
but rather for carrying on a sexual relationship with LeRae
Petersen.

Magdelena Luczak

Later, after the dust had settled on this terrible tragedy, there would be questions. How had this happened in a modern society? How was it possible that a four-year-old child could be systematically starved and tortured to death? Why had no one intervened? That there were no answers to these inquiries is a sad indictment on everyone involved.

Magdelena Luczek had moved to the UK from her native Poland in search of a better life. Born in the rundown city of Lodz in 1986, Magdelena had been raised in a grim concrete tower block, with her family of seven occupying a tiny apartment. Her father was a truck driver and was seldom home. Her mother, Yolanta was a housewife with a fierce temper who frequently beat her children. During the 24 years they lived in the building, the Luczek family never once paid rent. Effectively, they were squatters.

But, even from a young age, Magdelena had dreams of better things. She was obsessed with her appearance, with fashion, with makeup. As a girl, she dreamed of becoming a pop star but by her teens, she was earning a living in a more practical way. Neighbors would see her being picked up by a flashy car in the mornings and dropped off late at night. She was dressed to the nines, with expensive clothes, shoes, and makeup. There were also strange men calling on her at odd hours. They assumed that she was working as a prostitute.

By the late-2000s, however, things had changed significantly for Magdelena. She was involved in a steady relationship with a truck driver named Eryk Pelka and the mother of two young children. Poland had, in the intervening years, become a member of the European Union and that opened up new opportunities for the couple. In 2009, they moved to the UK, where they settled in the city of Coventry, in the English Midlands. There, Magdelena found work as a hotel cleaner and Eryk started working as a delivery driver.

It was a new beginning but one that would not last. Magdelena had always been a heavy drinker and, when she was drunk, she'd become argumentative and aggressive. She was also a frequent drug user. Eventually, Eryk could take no more. He walked out on the relationship and headed back to Poland, leaving the kids in Magdelena's dubious care. Soon, Magda would have a new man in her life, a bull-necked former soldier named Mariusz Krezolek.

Krezolek was, like Magda, a Polish national. His decision to move to the UK, though, had been forced, rather than voluntary. He was a wanted criminal in his homeland, one who had skipped out on a jail term after being caught driving under the influence for the umpteenth time. And these were not Krezolek's only offenses. He was a thug and a bully who had been dishonorably discharged from the Polish army for beating a fellow recruit to within an inch of his life. Now he had a new target for his violence, Magdelena's 4-year-old son, Daniel.

Why it was that Krezolek developed such enmity towards the child is not specifically known. Perhaps it was because Daniel had learning disabilities and may have been autistic. Whatever the reason, teachers at Coventry Little Heath Primary School began to notice that the boy was losing weight and frequently had bruises on his body. Once, he even came to school with two black eyes. He was displaying odd behavior too, stealing food from his classmates' lunchboxes and, when those were locked away from him, rummaging through garbage bins on the school property, looking for scraps of food.

Magdelena was asked about this of course, but she had her answers all lined up. She explained the bruises by saying that Daniel was a clumsy child who often fell while playing. His weight loss and perpetual hunger, she said, were due to a genetic eating disorder for which he was taking medication. She then warned the teachers not to feed him, since this would interfere with his treatment. To their eternal shame, they accepted these outlandish explanations.

But the teachers at Little Heath were not the only ones to be hoodwinked by Magdelena Luczek. In January 2011, Daniel was taken to a local hospital with a broken arm. It was an extremely clean break, as though the arm had been deliberately snapped against a counterpoint. Certainly, it did not fit the mother's explanation that the child had been jumping on a couch and had fallen. The hospital therefore called in Social Services but Magdelena became so aggressive when they started questioning her, that they let the matter drop.

And so, Daniel Pelka was returned to his mother and the torture continued. The little boy was systematically starved, he was beaten, he was forced to eat salt. At night, he was locked in a tiny bathroom where he had to sleep on a soiled mattress. If he wet the bed, as he frequently did, he was subjected to military-style punishments. Despite his weakened condition, he was made to run on the spot or perform squats until he collapsed from exhaustion. A few months short of his fifth birthday, he weighed just 23 pounds, the same as an 18-month-old baby. Malnutrition had stunted his bone development and he stood just 3ft 3inches tall, six inches smaller than the average. His body was marked by bruises and injuries, some old, some recently inflicted.

The abuse meted out to this innocent child was horrific beyond belief. It could not continue indefinitely. There is only so much that the human body can endure. At 3:07 a.m. on the morning of March 3, 2012, Mariusz Krezolek dialed 999 and summoned urgent medical help. Paramedics were at the address he provided within seven minutes but they were too late. Daniel's emaciated body was cold to the touch. His lips had already turned blue. He was transported to Coventry's University Hospital where death was formally pronounced at 3:50 a.m.

Questioned about the child's death, Krezolek and Luczak trotted out their standard cover story about a rare eating condition. They said that Daniel had been "feeling bad" all day and had "suddenly stopped breathing." But the doctors who had attended to the child knew that this was untrue. They had already concluded that the little boy had died of a brain aneurysm, caused by a blow to the head. Despite their denials, both Magdelena Luczak and Mariusz Krezolek were arrested and charged with murder.

Luczak and Krezolek would continue to repudiate their guilt when the matter came to trial in July 2013. But the evidence was strongly against them. There were the autopsy results which showed thirty separate injuries, clear evidence of malnutrition, and signs of systematic abuse. There was a computer taken from the apartment with telltale searches like, "table salt overdose," "when a child stops responding," and "patient in a coma." There were incriminating texts that had passed between the co-accused. There were Krezolek's boasts to co-workers about his mistreatment of Daniel.

Who had inflicted the actual harm? Since each blamed the other, that is impossible to say for certain. However, the ultimate blame must rest with Magdelena Luczak. She was the child's mother. It was her responsibility to ensure his wellbeing.

Asked why she had failed in this basic parental duty, Luczak at first said that she had gone along with Krezolek because she was afraid of him. But the texts that she'd exchanged with her lover proved otherwise. In them, she admitted to beating Daniel, to nearly drowning him in the bathroom, to depriving him of food, to force-feeding him with salt. It was also she who had held back on summoning help after Daniel suffered his head injury. She had sent a text to Krezolek saying that Daniel would "be okay in the morning." But for that delay, the boy's life might have been saved.

Luczak would later provide an alternate explanation for her participation in her son's torture and murder. She now placed the blame on "her obsessive love for Mariusz," her alcoholism, and her use of amphetamines and cannabis. As though any of this justified what she had done to the little boy.

In the end, it took the jury just under four hours to find Magdelena Luczak and Mariusz Krezolek guilty of murder. They each received a life sentence, with a minimum tariff of thirty years. The case sparked widespread outrage across the UK. Even Deputy Prime Minister Nick Clegg weighed in, calling the murder "vile" and "evil." Inevitably, there was an inquiry into the failure of the school, health professionals, and social services to identify Daniel as a victim of child abuse. But no one lost their jobs. Daniel Pelka had been badly let down.

Ana Trujillo

The victim had been stabbed to death with a stiletto. No, not the long, slim-bladed dagger favored by mobsters and hitmen but the five-and-a-half-inch heel of a stylish, blue suede pump, size nine. The person who had wielded this makeshift weapon was 45-year-old divorcee, Ana Trujillo. The man she'd killed was her former boyfriend, University of Houston medical researcher, Dr. Alf Stefan Andersson. Ana was claiming self-defense. The evidence at the bloody crime scene pegged her as a liar.

Ana Trujillo and Stefan Andersson made a most unlikely couple. He was a cultured, educated, and soft-spoken man; she was a brash and gregarious spitfire, a hard-drinking party girl who had moved to Houston from Waco, Texas, after dumping her two kids with her mother. Their only point of commonality was a mutual love of the bottle. Stefan was an alcoholic who spent his evenings drinking at the upscale bars of Houston's Museum District. It was here, in the Fall of 2012, that he met Ana Trujillo. The attractive brunette walked right up to him and demanded a drink. Flattered by the attention, Stefan complied. The two of them spent the rest of the night drinking together and ended up back at Stefan's luxury high-rise apartment. After that, Ana moved in. It is unclear whether Stefan invited her or if she simply installed herself in his life.

Whatever the case, Dr. Andersson would soon learn that his new girlfriend was not the most convivial of roommates. Ana had a temper and it was at its worst when she'd been at the bottle. She was an angry drunk, verbally and sometimes physically abusive when she had a drink in her. Stefan tolerated this behavior for six months, ignoring the pleas of friends who urged him to break off with Ana. A mild-mannered and easygoing man, he would continue to put up with Ana's aggression for six months before he finally reached his break point. In May 2013, he told her that it was over and asked her to move out. Ana responded initially with tears. By the time she walked out, lugging her suitcase, those tears had been supplanted by curses and threats of violence.

Ana's next stopping point was with an ex-lover, James Wells. James had since moved on with his life and was living with his new girlfriend. However, Ana soon turned on the waterworks, saying that she had nowhere else to go. The couple took pity on her and let her stay. That would turn out to be a bad mistake. Ana had promised to be on her way within a few days but days turned into weeks with no sign that she intended leaving anytime soon. Not only that but she was a far from agreeable houseguest. She was frequently drunk and often aggressive towards her hosts. The tipping point came when she attacked James and bit him on the scalp after drunkenly accusing him of making fun of her. This was

not a cursory attack, either. It drew blood and might have been
even worse had James's girlfriend not come to his aid, beating Ana
off with a broomstick. She was back on the street that same night.

And who did Ana turn to in her hour of need? The ever-reliable
Stefan, of course. Stefan was none too pleased when she showed
up on his doorstep, but he was a considerate man. He caved in as
soon as Ana started crying, telling him that she would have to
sleep on the streets if he didn't help her. She swore that it would
only be for a couple of days, just the time she needed to finalize a
few things and buy a bus ticket back to Waco. That was when
Stefan stepped aside and let her in.

Ana was on her best behavior over the two days that she
cohabitated with her ex. She was true to her word too. On June 9,
2013, she arrived home to show Stefan the Greyhound ticket she'd
booked for the next day. Now Stefan felt bad for doubting her
intentions. To make things up to her, he suggested a farewell
dinner which Ana gladly accepted. The meal was pleasant and the
pair left the restaurant feeling a little tipsy after consuming a
couple of bottles of wine. But tipsy just wouldn't cut it with heavy
drinkers like Ana and Stefan. Their next stop was at one of their
favorite bars where they continued drinking well into the night.

By the time they left, ejected at closing time, Ana Trujillo was in a
belligerent mood. First, she unleashed an expletive-laced tirade at
bar staff. Then she diverted her anger to the taxi driver who
picked them up. Then she turned on Stefan, becoming so
aggressive in the back of the cab that the driver expressed
concerns for Stefan's safety as he was paying her. He assured the

cabbie that it would be okay, that Ana was just blowing off steam. Then he headed upstairs.

It was now just after 2 a.m. Stefan Andersson had had a lot to drink and just wanted to pass out on his bed and sleep it off. But Ana was still drinking and still spitting fire. She rounded on Stefan, flinging insults and threatening violence. Eventually, Stefan who'd never so much as lifted a finger towards her during their relationship, grew tired of the tirade. He asked her to leave, not in the morning but now, immediately. That was when things turned nasty.

Ana's initial onslaught was with her fists, her open hand, her nails. Stefan parried these blows but did not respond with any of his own. He was not the kind of man to use violence, least of all against a woman. Instead, he retreated, turned his back and ran towards his bedroom, where he could lock himself in, away from this crazy woman. Unfortunately, he lost his footing in the hall and fell.

Ana, following close behind, was on him in a flash. As Stefan tried to rise, she pinned him, flat on his back, to the carpet. Then she reached behind her and removed one of her shoes. The stiletto heel had a steel support rod running through it. In Ana's hands, it became a deadly weapon. Blow after vicious blow was landed, the slim heel penetrating the flesh and bone of Stefan's head and neck, inflicting terrible damage. The coroner would later count 25 separate injuries. Many of them would have been fatal on their own.

At 3:45 a.m., a Houston 911 dispatcher fielded a call from a woman who claimed that she had been attacked and needed help. Units were dispatched to the address that Ana Trujillo gave and arrived to find Dr. Stefan Andersson dead on the floor, his features so thoroughly obliterated that the officers initially thought he'd been shot in the face. Trujillo's story was that Stefan had attacked her and that she'd been forced to defend herself. But no one who looked down on the mutilated corpse was ever going to believe that story. A single blow might have been construed as self-defense but two dozen was cold-blooded murder. Ana Trujillo left the apartment complex in handcuffs that night.

And yet, Trujillo continued to peddle her self-defense story, right into the trial. Her story was that Stefan had gripped her in a 'bear hug,' that she was being suffocated, that she'd have died had she not acted. But this simply did not gel with the evidence. Ana had been examined by a doctor shortly after her arrest and was found to be uninjured, with not so much as a bruise on her. The "life-threatening" situation she had described, had left her totally unmarked. Friends, family, and colleagues also testified as to Stefan Andersson's character. This was a man who abhorred violence and avoided confrontation at all costs. By contrast, there were a slew of witnesses who spoke of Ana Trujillo's aggressive tendencies, including her ex-boyfriend James Wells and a security guard she'd attacked at her workplace. By the end of this testimony, the jury was left with little doubt as to who the aggressor had been.

Found guilty of murder, Ana Trujillo was sentenced to life in prison on April 11, 2014. Parole was not ruled out but Trujillo must serve at least 30 years before she is eligible. She will be in her 70s by the time she qualifies for release. Given that she still refuses to acknowledge responsibility for Stefan Andersson's death, she may well die behind bars.

Liz Golyar

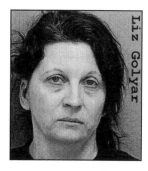

When 37-year-old Shana 'Liz' Golyar met single dad, Dave Kroupa, in an Omaha, Nebraska nightclub in 2012, it wasn't exactly love at first sight. Liz didn't roll that way. She was a party girl, a free spirit, a liberated woman. This was hardly her first rodeo. And Dave was happy with that. Recently emerged from a messy breakup, the last thing he wanted was another entanglement. What Dave had in mind was uninhibited, no-strings-attached sex. That just happened to be Liz's favorite kind.

But here's the thing with open relationships. They only work while both of the individuals involved are happy to keep them that way. Just a few weeks into the fling and Liz was decidedly unhappy with the status quo. She'd fallen hard for Dave and wanted him all to herself. Unfortunately for Liz, Dave didn't share her enthusiasm for a committed relationship. In fact, he'd just added another woman to his harem.

Cari Lea Farver was the same age as Liz Golyar and of similar disposition when it came to sex. She was playing the field, looking for casual gratification with no lasting commitments. But Cari was a very different person to Liz. Where Liz was brash, Cari was demure; where Liz was impulsive; Cari was calm and centered. Dave Kroupa must have found these character traits appealing because he soon found himself falling for her. Despite Cari's insistence that she wasn't ready for a monogamous relationship, Dave decided to devote himself to winning her heart. For that to happen, Liz had to go. Dave told her that it was over.

But Liz Golyar was not the kind of woman to step graciously aside. Rather than fade into the background, she began stalking her rival, inundating her with calls and texts, warning her to stay away from "her man." When these threats failed to have the desired effect, she decided on a different approach, creating a series of fake social media profiles and taking her campaign online. Cari found herself flooded with hundreds of abusive posts. It seemed to do the trick.

On Tuesday, November 13, 2012, Dave Kroupa received a text from the woman he'd fallen in love with, telling him that she never wanted to see him again. That same day, Cari tendered her resignation to her employer, again via text. There were texts to her family too, informing them that she was leaving town and moving to Kansas City, telling them not to try contacting her. She needed time and space, she said.

This sudden shift in behavior was utterly baffling to Cari's inner circle. It was so unlike the loving, caring woman they knew, to just drop out of their lives without explanation. But Cari hadn't

disappeared entirely. She seemed to have developed a decidedly
malicious streak. Suddenly, Dave Kroupa found himself swamped
with hostile messages, sent from a social media account bearing
Cari's name. His property was also vandalized and he wasn't alone
in this. Liz Golyar was also being threatened, warned that her
house would be burned to the ground with her in it and that her
pets would be killed. Eventually, Dave and Liz went to the Omaha
police and filed charges of harassment and stalking. They'd file
several more over the years that followed. These complaints
remained open but unresolved, however, since the police were
unable to track down the alleged perpetrator.

The campaign of intimidation carried out by Cari Farver had one
other effect on the lives of the people involved. Drawn together by
the harassment they'd been subjected to, Dave and Liz began
seeing each other again. But this wasn't the relationship that Liz
had hoped for. To Dave it was still about casual sex. Liz would
break it off several times, hoping to force his hand. She always
returned when she realized that Dave didn't care, one way or the
other. So perhaps it hadn't been about Cari, after all. Perhaps there
was another threat.

In December 2014, Liz Golyar showed up at an Omaha police
station and filed a complaint, alleging that she was being harassed
by a woman named Amy Flora. Amy was the mother of Dave
Kroupa's children and the two remained on good, if not intimate,
terms. According to Liz, Amy had been sending her abusive texts
and messages. She also said that she was afraid of Amy. Dave
Kroupa's gun had recently gone missing and Liz suspected that
Amy had taken it. She was convinced that Amy intended using it

against her. Those fears turned out to be well-founded. That very same night, Liz Golyar was shot.

The shooting happened at Big Lake Park, where Liz had gone to reflect on the trauma that Amy Flora was putting her through. But Amy had followed her to the park and approached in the darkness holding a gun. She commanded Liz to lie on the ground and then fired a single shot, hitting Liz in the thigh and narrowly missing her femoral artery. Half an inch to the left and Liz would have been killed. As it was, she'd survived to name her attacker. Now, she wanted Amy arrested.

Unfortunately for Liz, the police didn't believe her story. It was clear from the trajectory of the bullet that the wound could not have been inflicted in the way she'd described. In fact, investigators were pretty certain that she'd shot herself. And if that was the case then what else might she be lying about? Had she been lying about the campaign of intimidation against her? If so, to what purpose? Might she know something about the strange disappearance of Cari Farver? Investigators were beginning to believe that she did. To unravel the mystery, they decided on an unusual strategy. They decided to string Liz along, hoping that she would entrap herself in the process.

The plan was simple. Liz was told that the police were investigating Amy Flora for the possible homicide of Cari Farver and asked for her help in exposing Amy as the killer. She willingly took the bait. Over the months that followed, she forwarded dozens of threatening messages to investigators, messages that came from social media accounts in Amy Flora's name. Then the police played another card and revealed (falsely) that some of Cari's remains had been found. That was when Liz offered up her theory of how Cari had been killed. She theorized that Amy had abducted Cari from her home and driven to a remote location. There she'd been stabbed, her body burned and dismembered and later disposed of in various dumpsters.

The level of detail that had been put into the description of the homicide, convinced the investigators more than ever that Liz Golyar was the person responsible. The problem was that they couldn't prove it, not without a corpse, a crime scene, or some other evidence that would tie Golyar to the murder. That was when they caught a lucky break. During a conversation with Dave Kroupa, they learned that he had a computer tablet that Golyar had left at his house while they were dating. He willingly handed this over and it was thus that the police finally gained the evidence they needed. The device contained hundreds of messages posted by Golyar. In some, she was the recipient, in others the sender. The sending accounts were in the names of Cari Farver and Amy Flora.

Golyar was computer savvy and had used VPNs and proxy servers to mask her trail. But computer experts soon hacked these communications. They also discovered something else on the device, something more macabre and far more incriminating. Among the thousands of photographs that Golyar had taken, were several that looked like decomposing human remains. One of these was a gruesome image of a dismembered foot. There was a rather unique tattoo etched on the dead flesh, the Chinese symbol for "mother." Cari Farver had just such a tattoo.

Pulling the strands together, the police believed that they now knew what had happened to Cari. They believed that she had died on November 13, 2012, the day of her disappearance. Liz had shown up at Cari's house that day and managed to talk her way in. She'd then drawn a knife and coerced Cari into revealing the passwords for her various accounts. Then she'd forced the unfortunate woman at knifepoint into her car.

The journey had taken them to a remote location and it was here that Cari was stabbed. Two wounds were inflicted, to the stomach and to the chest. The latter was fatal. Liz then doused the body with gasoline and set it alight. However, she'd soon learned that destroying a corpse by fire is no easy task. In the end, she had to resort to the gruesome task of dismemberment. Cari's body parts ended up in various landfills. The only reason the police were able to construct such a detailed recreation was because of Liz's "confession."

In the aftermath of the murder, Liz initiated the cruel charade of assuming Cari's online identity. First, she contacted Dave Kroupa and broke off their relationship. Then she sent a resignation text to Cari's employers. The next message went to Cari's family, telling them that she was moving away and didn't want to be contacted. She would keep up back-and-forth communications with certain family members for years thereafter.

Had Liz left it at that then she might well have gotten away with murder. But she now decided to turn Dave against Cari and also to portray herself as a victim. That ploy worked so well that she later tried a similar tactic to eliminate another rival for Dave Kroupa's affection – Amy Flora. Her plan wasn't to kill Amy but to frame her for murder, a murder that she had committed. In the end, that would be her downfall.

Shanna 'Liz' Golyar was convicted of first-degree murder and second-degree arson in August 2017. She was sentenced to life in prison with no possibility of parole. The 20-year term that was added for the arson conviction made little difference. She is never getting out of prison. Cari Farver's body has never been found.

Vicky Efandis

Consider for a moment the fate of the male Latrodectus spider. For this unfortunate creature, every sexual encounter might be his last. The female Latrodectus (more commonly known as the Black Widow) is larger than the male, more venomous, more aggressive. She is also inclined to cannibalism. The male needs to be pretty fleet-footed, lest he become lunch once copulation is completed.

Similarly, in the human realm, there is a genus of female killer who displays a distinctly homicidal tendency towards males. Borrowing the name 'Black Widow' from their arachnid counterparts, these killers are usually financially motivated and are quite prepared to kill to achieve their aims. Their modus operandi is usually to lure, seduce, fleece, and then kill their victims. A prime example is Australian Vasiliki "Vicky" Efandis.

Like most of us, George Marcetta had good things and bad things in his life. The 56-year-old divorcee ran a successful painting and decorating business in Melbourne, Australia. He lived in a comfortable home in the suburb of Dandenong, about 18 miles south of the city center. He was financially well off. George, though, was lonely. He'd been alone since his divorce and longed for someone with whom he could share his good fortune.

But George was under no illusions. He wasn't a particularly handsome man and probably looked older than his years. He wasn't sophisticated either or a great conversationalist. Certainly, he was not the kind of man to sweep a lady off her feet. Still, he yearned for female companionship, someone to come home to at night, someone to have and to hold. With his twilight years fast approaching, he feared that the chance of love might have passed him by.

But then there was Vicky Efandis. Vicky came swooping into George's life when he hired her as a house cleaner in 2002. At 44, she was twelve years younger than George and quite attractive. Inexplicably, she also appeared to be interested in him. She'd barely been on the job a few days when George got the distinct impression that she was flirting. That emboldened him enough to ask her to dinner. He was astonished when she said yes. They ended the night in bed together. From that moment on, George was firmly on the hook. He fell hard and heavy for his younger lover, surrendering himself to her completely.

George Marcetta had not gained his particular station in life by being a fool. He was a shrewd businessman and a tough wheeler-dealer. But where Vicky was concerned, George was a putz. She was soon manipulating him, spinning an ever-expanding web which George seemed powerless to escape. In no time at all, he'd made her a 50% stakeholder in his business. Then Vicky complained that she didn't like the Dandenong house and George agreed to sell it. The new property he bought in Bellfield was solely in Vicky's name. She even convinced him to register his new Jaguar motor vehicle in the name of her daughter.

George's friends, meanwhile, noticed other changes in him. George had always been a generous man, willing to help out those in need. Now, when one of his friends asked him for a short-term loan, George said that he would have to clear it with Vicky first. The friend never heard back from him. Quite obviously, Vicky had given the thumbs down.

To everyone in George's circle, it was obvious that Vicky was a schemer, that she was using him, fleecing him. Yet what offense had she committed? George's friends might have disliked her but it was his money to do with as he pleased. And if he was disposed to sharing his wealth with the woman he loved, who were they to criticize?

The problem was that George's friends were right about Vicky. She had no real affection for George. To her, he was a meal ticket, no more, no less. George was not the first wealthy, older man she'd latched on to. She had a history of similar relationships. Usually, she'd love them and leave them, a little bit older, a little bit poorer, a little bit more cynical perhaps. In the case of George Marcetta, though, Vicky was going nowhere. If anyone was leaving, it would have to be George.

On the night of Wednesday, September 8, 2004, firefighters were summoned to a house in Bellfield and arrived to find a fierce conflagration that had all but engulfed the property. So ferocious was the blaze that it took the fire teams over an hour to bring it under control. When they were finally able to enter the property, they discovered one casualty, lying on the bed in the master bedroom. George Marcetta had died with his house.

George Marcetta's charred body was taken to the morgue for autopsy. In the meantime, fire department investigators got to work trying to determine the cause of the blaze. They soon found evidence of foul play. Accidental house fires almost always have a single point of origin. In this case, the blaze had sprung up in several places at once, a most unlikely scenario. Also, there was evidence that an accelerant, possibly kerosene, had been used. Then the results of George's autopsy were in and confirmed what the investigators suspected. Traces of Serapax, a powerful sleeping pill, were found in the dead man's bloodstream. It appeared that George had been drugged and that the house had been set on fire as he slept. He had been burned alive.

But who might have done such a horrible thing? The obvious suspect was Vicky Efandis, who stood to gain considerably from George's demise. Vicky appeared both distraught and perplexed when informed of her lover's death. "But I just spoke to him," she said. She then explained that she'd visited George the previous evening and had sent him a text to say goodnight when she had reached her home in nearby Ivanhoe. George had texted her back, returning the greeting.

Vicky's purpose in sharing this trivial detail was blatantly obvious to investigators. She was establishing an alibi, showing them that George had been alive and well when she'd left and that she could not possibly have started the fire. But Vicky had miscalculated badly in concocting her cover story. When detectives checked the cellphone records they did indeed find the texts that Vicky had referenced. However, both messages had been sent from the same location – the Bellfield house. Rather than deflecting suspicion, Vicky had turned the spotlight directly on herself. And the investigative team would soon uncover further incriminating evidence – the fact that she had been prescribed Serapax; the fact that she had made several purchases of kerosene over the preceding months. In no time at all, Efandis found herself under arrest and charged with murder.

Vicky Efandis was brought to trial at the Victoria Supreme Court in 2008. She entered a not guilty plea but faced a strong, if mainly circumstantial, prosecution case. According to the state, Efandis had planned the murder for several months, evidenced by her stockpiling of 28 liters of kerosene. On the night of the murder, she fed George Marcetta his favorite dish, rolled pork and noodles, lacing it with several Serapax tablets. George ate the meal and began to feel drowsy. He soon retired to bed and passed out. Efandis then sent the text messages she'd later rely on to support her story. Then she walked through the house, pouring kerosene and starting fires in several locations. She left just as the flames were taking hold.

In response to these allegations, all that the defense could offer was that the prosecution case was circumstantial and not supported by eyewitness testimony or forensics that tied Efandis to the crime. That was never going to be a convincing enough argument. After deliberating for three days, the jury returned a guilty verdict. Vicky Efandis was sentenced to 24 years in prison and must serve at least 20 years before she is eligible for parole.

One haunting question remains unanswered about this case. How did George Marcotta actually die? Did he fail to wake from his drug-induced slumber? Was he quickly overcome by the smoke and asphyxiated? Or did the smoke and flames rouse him from sleep? Did he wake in the midst of an inferno? Was he aware of what was happening and yet too weak to act? Did he pay a price in terror for his brief romance with a heartless Black Widow?

Carole Tregoff

It has all the elements of a Hollywood film noir – greed, sex, deceit, and cold-blooded murder. Fans of that genre will also recognize the usual players – the unfaithful husband, the frigid wife, the femme fatale, the duplicitous hitman. The bungling nature of the conspirators in this case even allows for a smidge of dark humor. But this was no laughing matter. A life was cut short here. A woman died who didn't have to.

Let's begin at the beginning, with 18-year-old Carole Tregoff interviewing for a receptionist job at the West Covina Medical Center in Los Angeles in 1956. Tall and lithe, with carefully styled auburn hair, Carole was a stunner. After a successful interview, she'd soon learn that she wasn't the only attractive woman working at the clinic. Good looks seemed almost a pre-requisite for employment here and Carole soon learned why. Her employer, Dr. Bernard Finch, had a reputation as a lady's man. Office gossip had it that the married, 40-year-old doctor was sleeping with at least two of his nurses.

At first, Carole paid little mind to the rumors. She had her own problems to contend with, trapped in a loveless marriage with her high school sweetheart, Jimmy Pappa. But Carole got a whole lot closer to Dr. Finch when, after seven months at the clinic, she was promoted to become his secretary. Then, in February 1957, he invited her to lunch and, a week later, to dinner. Carole arrived home in the early morning hours from that date, leading to an argument with her husband which got physical. Jimmy Pappa resolved the altercation by slapping her in the mouth. From that point on, Carole never submitted to his conjugal demands again.

But while her marriage was on the rocks, Carole's relationship with her handsome employer was going from strength to strength. After weeks of flirting, Dr. Finch suggested that they might rent an apartment where they could "spend time together." Carole agreed. Thereafter, they would meet up at their little love nest before and after work and sometimes during their lunch break. This wasn't just casual sex either. Soon they were exchanging declarations of love and talking about divorcing their spouses.

For Carole, this was easy. Her marriage to Jimmy Pappa was over anyway, bar the shouting. For Dr. Finch, though, divorce was a far more intricate process. The good doctor was worth a reputed $750,000 and California's community property laws meant that he'd have to cede half of his fortune to his wife, Barbara, more if Barb could prove adultery. Dr. Finch declared himself willing to take the financial hit in the name of love, just not at this particular time. His clinic was still heavily leveraged. For now, Carole would have to be content with being the "other woman."

And this was a sacrifice that Carole was willing to make, especially once Dr. Finch explained the arrangement that he and his wife had in place. Their marriage was a sham, he claimed, kept up only for the sake of appearances. He and Barb might live under the same roof, they might attend their tennis club together and appear as a couple at cocktail parties, but that was where it ended. There was no intimacy. Barb had been sexually frigid since the birth of their son a few years earlier. Moreover, she was happy for him to seek his pleasure elsewhere, as long as he was discreet about it.

This would have made for a civilized arrangement between Dr. and Mrs. Finch, if only it were true. Unfortunately, it was not. Barb might have tolerated her husband's wandering eye but that didn't mean she had to like it. She first became aware of Bernard's interest in Carole Tregoff when she spotted him and Carole entering their love nest apartment, Bernard carrying a bagful of groceries. The doctor tried to explain that away by insisting that he was just helping out an employee who needed a ride to the store. But then Barb started noticing Carole at the tennis club and at social events. The stunning redhead wasn't easy to miss.

In September of 1958, Barbara Finch finally tired of her husband's excuses and decided to take action. Her strategy was one employed by wronged spouses the world over. She called Jimmy Pappa and told him that his wife was cheating. Jimmy was stunned. When Carole got home that night he confronted her and Carole coldly confirmed that it was true. She was done with him.

That very night, she packed up her things and left, moving in temporarily with her father. A few days later, Jimmy showed up at the clinic and confronted Dr. Finch, who outright denied any romantic interest in Carole. Jimmy left confused. The situation was made a whole lot clearer to him a few days later when Carole served him with divorce papers.

Bernard Finch had dodged a bullet in the altercation with his wife's lover. But he'd be less successful in managing his domestic situation. In January 1959, Barbara engaged a divorce attorney, Joseph Forno, and set the wheels in motion to end her marriage. Since she alleged adultery, Forno employed a private eye to follow Bernard around, hoping to catch him in the act with Carole. But the lovers were ultra-careful and the detective found nothing. When the papers were eventually filed, they would cite "extreme cruelty."

There was certainly evidence to support those grounds. In May 1959, Barbara Finch received several stitches to a gaping wound above her eye. She claimed that Bernard had pistol-whipped her; he said that she'd suffered a fall and hit her head on a coffee table. In any case, it was the last straw. The Finches separated on May 18. On May 20, divorce papers were filed. The following day, Barbara obtained a restraining order, preventing her husband from molesting her and from disposing of any assets. At the same time, Finch was ordered to pay $2,000 in legal fees, $500 in court costs, and $200 a month alimony to his estranged wife.

With things hotting up in the Finches' divorce, Bernard and Carole decided mutually that it might be best for Carole to remove herself from the scene until the dust of the battle had settled. On May 26, Carole moved to Las Vegas, into an apartment paid for by her lover. Bernard would often visit her here and when he wasn't around, she filled in her time by working as a cocktail waitress. It was through this job that she met another key player in the melodrama, a low-rent gigolo named John Patrick Cody.

The initial idea was for Cody to travel to Los Angeles where he would seduce Barbara Finch. He'd then appear at the divorce trial to testify as to the indiscretion, thus swinging things in Bernard's favor. But Cody had a better idea. Why would Dr. Finch want to share his fortune when he could keep it all? Why not just remove his wife from the equation? The ex-con swore that he had carried out hits before and would do it for a cut-price $1,200, plus expenses. It took very little persuasion for Dr. Finch to agree.

With a $350 down payment, and an airline ticket in hand, Cody departed, ostensibly to carry out the hit. A few days later he returned, declared that it was done, and pocketed the agreed-upon balance of $850. Then Dr. Finch called Carole from L.A. and told her that his wife was not dead but very much alive. Confronted about this, Cody feigned surprise and asserted that he must have killed the wrong woman. He also weaseled another few hundred dollars out of Carole so that he could return to California to rectify his mistake. Thereafter, he promptly disappeared. The next time Dr. Finch and Carole encountered him, was in a courtroom, where he appeared as a prosecution witness.

John Patrick Cody had failed to carry out the hit he'd been paid for but he had planted an idea in the minds of Bernard Finch and

Carole Tregoff. Barbara's death would solve a lot of problems, leaving them unencumbered and a whole lot richer. And if the job had to be done, then it was best kept in-house. They'd already been burned by Cody. They weren't going down that path again.

On the evening of July 18, Finch and Carole drove in Carole's car to the country club near the Finch home, where they parked the vehicle. They then proceeded on foot to the opulent Lark Hill Drive residence, arriving to find the garage empty. Barbara wasn't home and so they sat down, out of sight, to wait. It was around 11:15 p.m. when Barbara drove up and pulled her car into the garage. Finch then walked in after her, while Carole remained hidden in the bushes.

Moments later, Barbara started screaming for help. A young au pair employed by the Finches heard the cry and came running towards the garage to investigate. As she did, there was a shot, and then Barbara was running, fleeing the garage with her husband in close pursuit. She did not make it far. Another shot perforated the night air and Barbara spilled face-first into the lawn, a dark stain spreading across her back.

By now, the police were on their way, summoned by the terrified au pair, Marie Anne Lindholm. They arrived too late to save Barbara Finch. Barb was dead, killed by a single .38-caliber bullet to the back. It was obvious who had killed her. Bernard and Carole had become separated in the confusion and would make their way separately back to Vegas, Carole in her car, Bernard in a couple of stolen vehicles. They were arrested within days and charged with murder.

Bernard Finch's defense at trial was an interesting one. He denied outright that he had killed his wife, contradicting the testimony of the au pair who had seen him in the garage. But Bernard's denial was undermined by a crucial piece of evidence. He'd dropped his briefcase at the crime scene. Inside, the police found two pairs of rubber gloves, a length of rope, a butcher knife, sedatives, a hypodermic, .38-caliber ammunition, and a flashlight. This was dubbed by one detective as a "do-it-yourself murder kit." Fitting the pieces together, prosecutors contended that Finch and Tregoff had arrived at the house that night, planning to subdue and sedate Barbara, load her into her car, and then push that car from the cliff near the Finch residence. This elaborate murder plot had been undone by the presence of Marie Lindholm. That had allowed Barb to flee, only to be gunned down as she tried to make her mistake.

On the face of it, this looked like an open and shut case. Yet there would be two mistrials before Finch and Tregoff were finally convicted, he of first-degree murder, she of second-degree. Both were sentenced to life imprisonment but would serve the bare minimum mandated by law. Carole Tregoff was paroled in 1969, after just eight years behind bars. She subsequently changed her name and moved to the Pasadena area. Bernard Finch was released two years later and moved to Missouri, where he practiced medicine for a decade before returning to California in 1984.

For more True Crime books by Robert Keller visit:

http://bit.ly/kellerbooks

Printed in Great Britain
by Amazon

40080853R00075